MISSION
PANDA RESCUE

Today fewer than 1,900 giant pandas, like this cub in China, remain in the wild.

MISSION PANDA RESCUE

ALL ABOUT PANDAS AND HOW TO SAVE THEM

KITSON JAZYNKA WITH NATIONAL GEOGRAPHIC EXPLORER DANIEL RAVEN-ELLISON

WASHINGTON, D.C.

>>CONTENTS

Pandas learn at a young age how to hang on to trees. It's a vital survival skill for the endangered species.

NATIONAL GEOGRAPHIC KIDS
MISSION ANIMAL RESCUE
Save ANIMALS Save the WORLD

Lions and *Tigers* and *Polar Bears*—oh, my! Be sure to check out the other titles in the Mission Animal Rescue series. Available on bookshelves near you.

MISSION ANIMAL RESCUE

At National Geographic we know how much you care about animals. They enrich our planet—and our lives. Habitat loss, hunting, and other human activities are threatening many animals across the globe. The loss of these animals is a loss to humanity. They have a right to our shared planet and deserve to be protected.

With your help, we can save animals—through education, through habitat protection, and through a network of helping hands. I firmly believe the animals of the world will be safer with us on their side.

Throughout this book and the other books in the Mission Animal Rescue series, you'll see animal rescue activities just for kids. If you go online at natgeo.com/kids/mission-animal-rescue, you can join a community of kids who want to help animals as much as you do. Look for animal rescue videos, chats with explorers, and more. Plus, don't miss the dramatic stories of animal rescues in *National Geographic Kids* magazine.

We share our Earth with animals. Helping them means helping our planet and protecting our future. Together we can do it.

—Daniel Raven-Ellison, *Guerrilla Geographer and National Geographic Explorer*

YOUR PURCHASE SUPPORTS ANIMALS AND THEIR HABITATS

The National Geographic Society is a nonprofit organization whose net proceeds support vital exploration, conservation, research, and education programs. Proceeds from this book will go toward the Society's efforts to support animals and their habitats. From building bomas for big cats to protect their wild territory to studying elephants and how they communicate to exploring wild places to better understand animal habitats, National Geographic's programs help save animals and our world. Thank you for your passion and dedication to this cause. To make an additional contribution in support of Mission Animal Rescue, ask your parents to consider texting ANIMAL to 50555 to give ten dollars. See page 112 for more information.

Captive pandas enjoy a crunchy meal of bamboo, a fast-growing woody plant.

HELP SAVE THE PANDA

What makes the giant panda such an irresistible animal? Its cuddly, docile appearance? Its humorous antics and its adorable black eye patches? Pandas have fascinated people since the animals first poked their unforgettable faces out of a rustling bamboo thicket. For centuries, giant pandas have been treasured as symbols of friendship and peace, yet humans have greatly reduced their natural habitat. Today, there are fewer than 1,900 pandas left in the wild. Deforestation not only impacts the places where pandas make their homes, it affects our entire planet. Researchers and zoos in China and around the world are working to maintain healthy panda populations in captivity to safeguard the species for the future. Conservationists are working to restore panda habitat. And by saving the panda and its forests, we're saving our own habitat, too.

All around the world, scientists, conservationists, and super-powered kids like you are observing and learning about these endangered animals and their disappearing habitat. The more we learn and share about the challenges pandas face, the better we can take steps to help protect this important species.

When it comes to conservation and saving pandas, age doesn't matter. Kids are an important part of the conservation puzzle and every effort counts. At the end of each chapter in this book, you'll find rescue challenges. By doing these activities, you'll learn more about pandas, the daily struggles they face, and how to spread the message about saving them.

So, what are we waiting for? Read on to learn how to make your voice heard. Let's save pandas!

Using her natural instincts, a mother carries her cub at the Wolong Panda Center in China's Sichuan Province.

THROUGH A PANDA'S EYES

A steady spring rain drips down the dense understory of a high mountain forest in China's Sichuan Province. Pink wild flowers suggest it's springtime, but it's cold in this bamboo forest. A male giant panda cub—just six months old and about the size of a golden retriever puppy—sits hidden in a bed of wet, leafy ferns. His thick, oily black-and-white coat seems impervious to the soaking rain.

GOOD INSTINCTS

The adorable young panda relaxes on his plush rump. With his legs stretched out in front of him, his furry forearms grab a tall, fibrous bamboo stalk. Already skilled in how to manipulate the juicy grass, he bends it down and breaks off a stalk about three feet (0.9 m) long.

With a great chomp, he bites down. He cracks it with his molars. In no hurry, he chews and chews. Suddenly, a sound like a bleating sheep stops him. But it's nothing to worry about—it's his mother, Cao Cao, calling him. The cub rolls onto his feet, then pads through the slippery, cold mud toward the sound of her voice.

PANDA CUB IN THE WILD

Tao Tao's ability to communicate with his mother, Cao Cao, comes naturally. For the cub's entire life, she has been his lifeline, nurturing him and teaching him vital survival skills.

Tao Tao is part of a new program called wild training at the Wolong Panda Center, a research and breeding center in China's Wolong Nature Reserve. He needs his mom now, but he was born to be a great explorer. He has an epic journey ahead of him.

Wild training means that although Tao Tao was born in captivity, he's learning important skills from his mother that will allow him to live in the wild. Cao Cao does all the teaching, passing on ancient lessons about survival that she learned from her wild-born mother. She shows Tao Tao how to find food and shelter, and how to keep his coat free of bugs like blood-sucking leeches, ticks, and fleas. It's all part of a rewilding program developed by Zhang Hemin, the director of the Wolong center. It's designed to prepare captive pandas to be released into the wild.

NOW PLAYING!

NATIONAL GEOGRAPHIC

NATIONAL GEOGRAPHIC PRESENTS

PANDAS
THE JOURNEY HOME

sky 3D O3F NGPANDAFILM.COM

MOVIE STAR

Filmmaker Nicolas Brown's National Geographic documentary titled *Pandas: The Journey Home* shows the world how Tao Tao, a captive-born panda, honed his instincts, learned how to be wild, and successfully returned to his ancestral home.

Captive panda actors, like Shou Xi Xi, played a part in the National Geographic documentary *Pandas: The Journey Home* to help tell the rewilding story of the panda Tao Tao.

To prepare Tao Tao, he is kept from seeing or smelling humans. Cao Cao takes care of him in a protected two-acre (0.8-ha) forest enclosure. As the cub grows, his mother demonstrates how to climb trees and cross over creeks. She shows him where to sleep and how to interact with other pandas, and she teaches him how to avoid predators.

Sometimes Tao Tao challenges his mother. He lives up to his name, which means "naughty" or "mischievous." One day, he scoots up a tall tree before Cao Cao can pull him down by the scruff of his neck. Fearless, he climbs up 30 feet (9 m). That's about as high as a third-story window. Worried, Cao Cao dashes up another tree close by and barks at him until he comes down.

WILDER, STILL

At six months old, Tao Tao still has many lessons to learn. He and Cao Cao will move farther up the mountain to increasingly larger, more remote enclosures for the next stages of wild training. It's colder up there, and there are more wild animals in the area surrounding the enclosures, like boars, Asian black bears, and other giant pandas. Their protected section of the bamboo-rich forest—the largest is the size of 59 football fields—will allow Tao Tao and his mother to experience a wild setting while the scientists continue to monitor their health and safety.

But before they can move him, his keepers have to capture and secure him. They dress up in fuzzy panda suits that have been "perfumed" with panda pee and poop. This way, the panda cub won't become accustomed to the smell of humans. They gently place the cub in a large basket. One of the keepers will carry the heavy load on his back a mile (1.6 km) up a steep, slippery mountain path and leave him with his mother.

THE REAL WILD

Months go by. Tao Tao grows into a robust, 21-month-old cub weighing about 80 pounds (36 kg). Caregivers observe the pandas by video monitor. The pandas have also been outfitted with audio collars so caregivers can listen to the pandas' every move while they go about their business, undisturbed in their mountain home.

SCIENTISTS HAVE OBSERVED PANDA MOMS SWATTING THEIR CUBS IF THEY ARE TOO RAMBUNCTIOUS.

Even though Tao Tao thrives in his wild-like home, his caregivers worry about releasing him. They think about another panda, a male named Xiang Xiang, who went through a similar but less successful training program awhile back.

Xiang Xiang's three years of training—taught primarily by humans—hadn't prepared him for life in the wild. Released in 2006, he died about a year later, possibly from injuries suffered after a fight with another panda. His experience provided researchers with important information.

FINAL TEST

The panda's caregivers will do whatever they can to prepare Tao Tao for life in the wild. Before his release, he must pass one final test: Does the young panda know how to react to the presence of a predator?

Armed with fresh droppings and urine from a snow leopard in a zoo, Wolong staff members trudge up the treacherous mountain trail in their panda suits one more time. In addition to the smelly stuff, they bring a large stuffed animal that looks like a leopard.

American filmmaker Nicolas Brown and his crew join the steep hike. Brown wears a ghillie suit, a disguise that looks like a tree (that is, a tree carrying a heavy load of camera equipment). One cameraman wearing a panda suit climbs a ladder to get the perfect shot. The suits don't make it easy to breathe or maneuver up and down muddy ravines. But the disguises will help Tao Tao retain a crucial fear of humans after his release.

Cao Cao wears a radio collar so keepers can find her in the enclosure. They douse the stuffed leopard with scent and try to fade into the scenery. A little while later Tao Tao wanders by. The scent startles him. At the same time, the sound of a scary leopard snarl hisses from a recorder. Tao Tao jumps and runs up a tree.

He has passed the test.

Director Zhang smiles. Tao Tao has the reflexes of a wild panda. The hope is that after his release, he will find a mate and introduce a new bloodline into a small, isolated population in China's Liziping Nature Reserve in Sichuan Province. The reserve includes 50,000 acres (20,234 ha) of pristine bamboo forest, but only about 13 wild pandas inhabit the area. Now there will be one more.

CHAPTER 1
>> THE BAMBOO BEAR

"ON THIS EARTH, IF PANDAS CAN BE SAFE, THEN THE ENVIRONMENT CAN BE SAFE, AND THEREFORE HUMANS CAN BE SAFE."

—ZHANG HEMIN, DIRECTOR OF WOLONG NATURE RESERVE

Wild pandas munch on more than 60 types of bamboo, including pencil-thin arrow bamboo and thick umbrella bamboo.

The world's most beloved bamboo-eater, the roly-poly giant panda (*Ailuropoda melanoleuca*), is the familiar, black-and-white bear that headlines at zoos around the world. These widely photographed rock stars might look cuddly, but a full grown male panda can weigh up to 350 pounds (159 kg) and is as dangerous as any other wild animal with big teeth and claws, though giant pandas are not known to have ever attacked humans.

NATIONAL TREASURE

The popular panda—considered a national treasure in its home, China—has two personas. The adorable, pampered, and almost pet-like zoo panda eats homemade Popsicles, takes food from the hands of caregivers, and travels the world to spread the love of pandas everywhere. A zoo panda might live to be 35 years old.

The mysterious wild panda usually avoids humans and has a shorter life span. They might weigh 15 pounds (7 kg) less than a captive panda, but are also much tougher and more alert than a captive panda. A wild panda lives like any other undomesticated animal fighting for its survival.

One thing all pandas share, however, whether they live in captivity or in the remote mountains, is a taste for bamboo. Pandas devour the starchy grass—leaves, shoots, and stalks—munching away on the crunchy stuff for as many as 16 hours each day.

IRRESISTIBLE PANDAS

Famous for their black-and-white coloration, pandas' white bodies have broad stripes of black fur that cover their shoulders and legs, and they have patches over their eyes. Scientists debate the reason for the black-and-white markings, but most agree it provides camouflage in pandas' often snowy, dark, shadowy habitat. Their adorable appearance might also serve as a way for pandas to recognize each other, since the shape

PANDA FUR FEELS LIKE SHEEP'S WOOL.

A giant panda's wide nostrils sniff out smelly messages left by other pandas.

>> WHERE PANDAS LIVE

In China, pandas live in the wild, at panda centers, and at zoos.

0 — 200 miles
0 — 200 kilometers

CHINA

Beijing Zoo

Shaanxi Rare Wildlife Rescue and
Breeding Research Center, Louguantai

China Conservation and Research Centre
for the Giant Panda

Chengdu Research Base
of Giant Panda Breeding

Chongqing
Zoo

Fuzhou Panda
World

Taiwan

NORTH
AMERICA

Toronto,
Canada

Memphis,
U.S.A.

Washington, D.C.
U.S.A.

San Diego,
U.S.A.

Atlanta,
U.S.A.

Mexico City,
Mexico

Edinburgh,
United Kingdom

Brugelette,
Belgium

St.-Aignan,
France

EUROPE

Vienna,
Austria

Madrid,
Spain

ASIA

CHINA

Kobe,
Japan

Tokyo,
Japan

Wakayama,
Japan

Taipei,
Taiwan

AFRICA

Chiang Mai,
Thailand

Kuala Lumpur,
Malaysia

Singapore,
Singapore

SOUTH
AMERICA

0 — 3000 miles
0 — 3000 kilometers

AUSTRALIA

Adelaide,
Australia

ANTARCTICA

MAP KEY

■ Wild panda range   🐼 Panda center   ○ Zoo with a panda

A panda keeps its balance at a zoo
in Austria.

and size of their markings vary slightly.

On four paws, a giant panda (roughly the size and shape of an American black bear) can stand up to three feet (0.9 m) tall at the shoulder—that's about waist-high for a sixth grader. From the tip of a panda's nose to the end of its fluffy white tail, a male panda can stretch six feet (1.8 m) long. Females are slightly smaller.

A panda's round, wide-set ears sit atop its furry white head. Its wide, glossy black nose is one of its most important survival adaptations, the physical features that help a species survive. Its keen ability to smell is super important because pandas communicate with each other primarily by scent.

Without the smelly "love letters" pandas leave for each other, male and female pandas might not find each other within the narrow window of time they have for successful mating each year. A panda has a certain scent depending on its age and whether it's male or female.

A panda's keen sense of smell interprets the messages and also helps it avoid conflict with other pandas.

Other adaptations that help a panda survive include its thick, water-resistant fur that keeps it warm and dry in its cold, wet habitat. Its "pseudo-thumb" (meaning "fake thumb") is really an elongated wrist bone covered by soft, padded skin. Though it's not a true thumb, like humans have, the bone functions as a thumb and allows the panda to grab and manipulate bamboo with precision.

A panda's tail is another survival adaptation. It not only protects the scent-producing glands on its backside, but it also helps "paint" smelly messages on trees, shrubs, rocks, or anything else it can rub its tail and glands on, including the walls of a zoo enclosure.

PANDAS HAVE BEEN EATING BAMBOO FOR AT LEAST 2.5 MILLION YEARS.

A panda cub in China's Wolong Nature Reserve navigates dense bamboo forest.

ALL IN A DAY'S WORK

A panda forages for bamboo for most of the day. Here are some other things a panda might squeeze in on a typical day.

A mother panda licks her newborn cub and cuddles it while it sleeps, keeping it warm and creating an important bond.

A panda stops to smell a scented message left on the bark of a tree by another panda.

A female panda might make a den in the cavity at the base of an old tree.

A cub learns to climb a tree where it can wait for its mom safely while she eats bamboo.

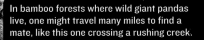

In bamboo forests where wild giant pandas live, one might travel many miles to find a mate, like this one crossing a rushing creek.

BAO BAO

On August 23, 2014, Bao Bao the giant panda cub dug her sharp claws into the giant number "1" on top of her birthday cake. Her caregivers at Washington, D.C.'s, Smithsonian's National Zoo concocted the icy, fruity confection—made of frozen, diluted apple juice and decorated with slices of apple and pear—to celebrate her first birthday. Bao Bao—her name means "precious treasure" in Chinese—slurped and licked the treat while fans crowded the railing around her enclosure. Her health and her first birthday represent years of successful collaboration between American and Chinese scientists trying to save pandas from extinction.

In honor of her birthday, the zoo, along with the Embassy of the People's Republic of China, held a Zhuazhou (ju-ah JO) ceremony—a traditional Chinese event held to honor a baby's first year. The tradition dictates that symbolic objects be placed in front of the baby—the one a panda chooses is said to foretell its future. Three symbolic posters had been painted for Bao Bao's ceremony. The 40-pound (18.1 kg) youngster chose a poster with a picture of a peach (a Chinese symbol for longevity) by nibbling on the paper and grabbing the bamboo stalk that held up the poster. After Bao Bao played with all three posters, she climbed up her favorite hemlock tree for a nap.

ANCIENT PANDAS

Giant pandas and their ancestors have been around for millions of years. The world is very different now from what it was in the time of the first pandas. To understand this time period on Earth, think woolly mammoths, woolly rhinoceroses, saber-toothed cats, giant ground sloths, and birds with 25-foot (7.6-m) wingspans. Although these animals have gone extinct, the giant panda remains. The species has survived ice ages and, so far, human degradation of its natural habitat.

Modern wild pandas have always lived in what is today central China. These days, the species survives only in the high elevations of central China's misty mountains. At elevations between 5,000 and 10,000 feet (1,524 and 3,048 m), the mixed coniferous and deciduous forest has a dense understory of almost impenetrable bamboo. Pandas once lived in lowland areas, too, but human development has left wild pandas only the more remote mountain areas.

Even though male pandas are known to fight during mating season—roaring as they fight for the right to be a father—they tend to avoid conflict. This may be due to the fact that they live in secluded areas and have plenty of time to retreat if threatened. Or perhaps it's because once a panda reaches sub-adult (or juvenile) size, it has no natural predators.

Giant pandas' avoidance of conflict may be simply because their food is so plentiful that they don't have to compete. They also don't hunt (unless you count wandering into a bamboo patch looking for the juiciest stalks as hunting). A giant panda would never hunt a moose or fight off a wolf for an elk carcass as a grizzly bear would, or snare a seal as a polar bear would.

>> ANIMAL RESCUE!

COOL UNDER PRESSURE

When Lun Lun the panda gave birth to twins at Zoo Atlanta in 2013, emotions ran high in the small, warm room adjacent to the panda's den. The team led by Dr. Rebecca Snyder had been on call for weeks. Even though they were prepared for twins, watching Lun Lun—an experienced mom—struggle to pick up and cradle her second cub sent them into emergency mode.

In the wild, if a mother delivers two babies, typically only one survives. If Lun Lun continued to struggle to care for both cubs, they might both die. In captivity in the United States, there had never been a case where both panda twins survived. Could Snyder lead the team to change that fact, and save these important newborns?

As a kid, Rebecca Snyder had watched her mom—a nurse—react quickly and calmly in any situation. As a panda conservationist, Snyder had studied panda moms skillfully caring for their cubs. She relied on those lessons to try and save the helpless cubs.

She had a plan. The team—the keepers, vets, and a skilled panda nursery keeper from China—channeled their worry into action. Using a padded hook prepared in advance, Snyder held her breath and gently pulled "Cub B" to a barred window in the birth den. Snyder's colleague Hayley Murphy summoned all of her courage, cupped the cub in her hands, and pulled it through the bars. She delivered it to a warm incubator ASAP.

Keepers covered the cub with a soft, warm cloth to mimic the feeling of Lun Lun's body. Soon they started the months-long process of swapping the cubs (taking turns between human caregivers and mom) so each one could nurse and bond with Lun Lun.

After weeks of intensive care, Cub B grew into a feisty cub. She was named Mei Huan and thrived, just like her sister, Mei Lun. Snyder felt confident that both cubs would grow up to be great mothers. But no matter how much time goes by, to Snyder, Mei Huan will always be that precious "Cub B" whose life she helped save.

Witnessing the birth of cubs like Yang Yang, born at the Chengdu Research Base of Giant Panda Breeding, and twins Mei Huan and Mei Lun, born at Zoo Atlanta. Then watching them grow and develop.

Rebecca Snyder records panda behavior at Zoo Atlanta in the U.S.A.

DR. REBECCA SNYDER

BORN: IOWA, U.S.A.
JOB TITLE: GIANT PANDA PROGRAM COORDINATOR, ZOO ATLANTA; AND ASSOCIATION OF ZOOS AND AQUARIUMS
LOCATION: ATLANTA, GEORGIA, U.S.A.
YEARS WORKING WITH PANDAS: 17

How are you helping to save pandas?
I study the behavior of giant pandas living in zoos and breeding centers. My research helps conservationists take better care of pandas. It also helps us understand what pandas need to mate, raise their cubs, and live long, healthy lives.

What's your favorite thing about your job?
I love to watch giant panda mothers take care of their cubs. For my research, I spend many hours watching or observing the giant pandas' behavior and writing down what they do.

What's the best thing about working in the field?
All of the scientists who study giant pandas work closely with each other and help each other. Sometimes science can be competitive and scientists in the same field don't work together. But with pandas, we know we can accomplish more by working together.

What's the worst thing about working in the field?
That I don't speak Chinese. I should have worked harder to learn Chinese because not only would it have made my work in China easier and more productive, I could have had more friendships with staff at the Chengdu Research Base of Giant Panda Breeding.

How can kids prepare to do your job one day?
Study math and science and learn to write well. A scientist has to be able to write to share what has been learned. Go to college and get a degree. Be compassionate and kind. These are important qualities for helping make the world a better place.

More than 300 pandas live in captivity in centers in China and zoos around the world.

ZOO PANDAS ARE OFTEN GIVEN FLATTERING NAMES, REPEATED FOR EMPHASIS, LIKE MEI MEI, WHICH MEANS "BEAUTIFUL."

BEAR-Y HUNGRY

All bears are classified in the scientific order Carnivora, and therefore are considered carnivores. All bears have the same simple digestive system adapted—like a dog's or a cat's—for eating meat. But while all bears' scientific classification is pure carnivore, they have omnivorous diets. That means bears, in general, eat mostly plants—like roots and berries—and some meat, like fish or mammals they can catch.

Pandas are 99 percent herbivorous (grass-eaters, like a horse). Yes, you read that right—and here's how it works: The giant panda is a carnivore by ancestry, but it's also an omnivore because it eats mostly plants (but also some meat). Then the grass-based diet of the giant panda (it's the only bear that survives almost entirely on grass) means that the species is also considered an herbivore.

Scientists consider a species with such a narrow dietary requirement to be a specialist. That means the animals require a specific set of resources, like bamboo for giant pandas or seals for polar bears (the only bear that eats meat as the majority of its diet), to survive and reproduce. The opposite of a specialist species is a generalist, like the wolf, a species that can survive almost anywhere and eat almost anything.

Specializing may have helped pandas outlive many species that have gone extinct during the millions of years giant pandas have existed on Earth. Abundant bamboo has functioned as a constantly charged evolutionary power source. Bamboo may not be the most nutritious food (pandas have adapted to it with special gut bacteria to digest the fiber-rich grass), but throughout the giant panda's evolution, it's a resource that has been available during every season and every era. Humans, however, have put a lot of pressure on bamboo forests, a precious resource that's critical for giant pandas' survival.

Misinformation has led some people to believe that pandas' specialization has caused the species to become endangered, but that's not the real deal. Pandas are endangered because of habitat loss due to human activities. Given protection and space in the proper wild habitat, they survive just fine.

A one-year-old panda cub scarfs down bamboo by the Pitiao River, which flows through China's Wolong Nature Reserve.

Panda expert Rebecca Snyder's tips for studying giant pandas:

1 A scientist, no matter what age, must be patient and wait to see interesting behaviors when observing pandas.

2 Have a good sense of humor—research can be time-consuming and sometimes frustrating.

3 Learn Chinese! Speaking the language makes it easier to study pandas in the wild and to work with Chinese scientists.

SAVING PANDAS

The names "giant panda," "panda bear," and plain old "panda" all refer to the same animal. Many scientists prefer the term "giant panda" because it's the most specific. The term "panda" alone could refer to the cute, raccoon-like, but unrelated, red panda. But no matter how you refer to the delightful giant panda, it's endangered, which means the animal is in danger of going extinct in the wild.

Some research indicates there are fewer than 1,900 in the wild. More optimistic scientists believe there might be as many as 3,000 pandas left in the wild—but the elusive animals are hard to count.

When scientists travel through panda territory, they see a lot more panda poop than pandas. They've used this smelly (and very abundant) resource to help tally populations of wild pandas—by sifting through panda poop and recording the length of bamboo stem fragments that they find. Each panda has fragments of distinctive lengths based on the size and placement of its teeth. Scientists also try to get a count of panda populations by DNA testing of the poop they find. No matter what, counting pandas is a tedious job and the results are not terribly accurate.

Today more than 300 pandas live in zoos and breeding centers around the world, mostly in China. In the United States, four zoos—Zoo Atlanta in Georgia, San Diego Zoo in California, Smithsonian's National Zoo in Washington, D.C., and Memphis Zoo in Tennessee—have giant pandas on loan from China.

Around the world, conservationists and zoos are helping to save endangered species like pandas by participating in global breeding programs. These breeding programs for endangered species help create genetic "insurance policies" for those animals still living in the wild, in case they become extinct. In the United States, the Association of Zoos and Aquariums has what it calls "Species Survival Plans" for many endangered species, from anteaters to zebras.

Zoos, especially those accredited by the Association of Zoos and Aquariums, provide environments for giant pandas that are as close to their natural home as possible. The animals educate millions of people about the lives and importance of pandas. Zoo webcams feed the insatiable appetite of people all over the world who want to go behind the scenes and explore the life of pandas.

The public's affection for pandas and the hard work of conservationists mean that the story of giant pandas is moving in a positive direction. Many people around the world are fighting to restore the diverse mountain habitat that's home to pandas—and other animals too, like the red panda, monkeys, and rare species of birds. Stories of conservation successes are featured in magazines and newspapers around the globe, filled with stories and irresistible images of pandas.

Heartwarming wildlife documentaries share the secrets of pandas' lives. Hundreds of nonprofit organizations have been formed around the world to protect pandas and educate the public about the importance of these wonderful bears.

You can help, too. There's no time to waste! The time is now. Let's save pandas!

Panda cubs snuggle up on a high ledge as they practice climbing.

>> RESCUE ACTIVITIES

LAUNCH A CAMPAIGN

Pandas need our help. You have the power to help protect pandas and other endangered wildlife. Pandas cannot campaign to save their habitat, but you can speak up for them. By reading this book and learning about pandas, you will have the expertise needed to raise awareness, support, and funds to help save this endangered species. Do this first challenge to get organized and launch your campaign.

MAKE A PLAN TO PROTECT PANDAS.

RAISE AWARENESS BY RUNNING AN EDUCATION CAMPAIGN. You could hold an art exhibition, make a video, or help people to learn about pandas in another way.

RAISE SUPPORT BY WRITING LETTERS OR PODCASTS. A well-written letter to a person in power can help wildlife, especially if it is signed by lots of people.

RAISE FUNDS TO PROTECT AND RESTORE PANDA HABITAT. Effective fund-raisers could include getting a sponsor, collecting donations, or selling panda-themed crafts.

BUILD A TEAM.

INVITE SOME FRIENDS TO FORM A TEAM. You can campaign as an individual, but the more of you there are, the more noise and excitement you will be able to create.

READ THIS BOOK TOGETHER AS A GROUP, plus check out articles, videos, and more from any other reliable source that interests anyone on your team. Meet to compare and review notes. By having the same level of expertise, you will be in a better position to think of ideas and answer questions.

COME UP WITH A STRONG NAME FOR YOUR CAMPAIGN, and decide how often you will meet and what you want to achieve. Agree on shared goals to make your campaign more successful.

SHARE YOUR CAMPAIGN NAME.

When people see your logo they should instantly be able to understand that you are campaigning to protect pandas.

when you explain your campaign, write letters, or make branded crafts. If it is catchy, people will remember what you are trying to achieve.

Grab an adult and go online, where you could launch a blog, Facebook page, or Twitter account to help amplify your message.

Here are some great tips for making a good team:

1

Agree on what you want to achieve. If you all have the same aim you are more likely to hit your target!

2

Give yourselves clear roles and responsibilities. That way you will all know who is doing what.

3

Listen to what each person on your team has to say and be willing to test out new ideas. It is very important that everyone feels involved.

"THERE IS A FEELING OF HOPE THAT THINGS ARE TURNING AROUND FOR GIANT PANDAS, AND THE SPECIES HAS A BRIGHTER FUTURE THAN IT DID 20 YEARS AGO."

—RON SWAISGOOD, PANDA BIOLOGIST

Surrounded by its favorite food, a panda munches on bamboo in China's Wolong Nature Reserve. A panda digests only about 17 percent of the bamboo that it eats.

CHAPTER 2

LAND OF PANDAS

Giant pandas' ancestry is not an easy subject to nail down. Science has not reached a final conclusion about the evolutionary path of our earliest bears and how they are related to the family of bears that exist today. The giant panda is one of eight members of the family Ursidae.

MEET THE BEAR FAMILY

Members of the bear species populate a diverse group of habitats around the Earth. Today two Ursidae species, the sloth bear (*Ursus ursinus*) and the smaller Southeast Asian sun bear (*Ursus malayanus*), live exclusively in southern subtropical forests in Asia, while four others—the giant panda, the polar bear (*Ursus maritimus*), American black bear (*Ursus americanus*), and brown bear (*Ursus arctos*)—live in the Northern Hemisphere. The Asian black bear (*Ursus thibetanus*) lives in southern subtropical forests but is also found as far north as Russia. The Andean bear (*Tremarctos ornatus*) lives in the Southern Hemisphere, primarily in the foothills of the Andes mountains in South America.

Scientists use Latin names to identify and classify organisms. It's called taxonomy. The names are identifiers, something like the name or number on the back of your soccer team shirt that identifies you.

Scientific names can help us determine who's a bear and who's not—like the red panda (*Ailurus fulgens*). Although the giant panda and red panda share a name, overlapping forest habitat in China, and a taste for bamboo, the red panda is more closely related to skunks and raccoons than to panda bears.

All bears are thought to have evolved from a group of plant- and meat-eating ancestors, referred to as *Ursavus,* that existed somewhere between 23 and 26 million years ago. Giant pandas were likely the first to branch off and form a separate species about 12 to 18 million years ago. One of the earliest ancestors of the

PANDAS MAY SEEM LAZY, BUT THEY ARE AGILE TREE-CLIMBERS AND SKILLED SWIMMERS.

Learning to climb is an essential survival skill for pandas in the wild.

panda was a bear-like animal that scientists named *Kretzoiarctos beatrix*, or *K. beatrix* for short—you'll read more about *K. beatrix* on page 35.

Many paleontologists believe that between two and three million years ago the Earth plunged into an Ice Age. This meant that things on the planet got much colder, but it was not necessarily covered in ice. In parts of China, where the panda's ancestors lived, bamboo thrived in cold temperatures. A smaller panda called *Ailuropoda microta* (it's also referred to as a pygmy panda) emerged, followed by the modern panda *Ailuropoda melanoleuca*. These two species had very similar bones and teeth and ate almost entirely bamboo.

HOME IS WHERE THE BAMBOO IS

Adapting its diet to the most abundant resource available—bamboo—helped ancient giant panda species survive. But in recent centuries, humans have taken away much of the bamboo forest that wild pandas now need to survive. Agriculture has restricted them to living high up in impenetrable bamboo forests across six isolated, earthquake-prone mountain ranges, which are central China's Qinling, Qionglai, Minshan, Liangshan, Daxiang Ling, and Xiaoxiang Ling mountains. The farming and development that overtook the area's lowlands has gradually crept upward, leaving only the steepest mountain ravines and ridges undeveloped by humans.

>> FAMILY TREE

Giant pandas have been roaming Asia for millions of years. All species of bears descended from a common ancestor—the mighty *Ursavus*.

Genus:
URSAVUS
As old as
23 MILLION
years ago

K. BEATRIX

24 MIL   21 MIL   18 MIL   15 MIL   12 MIL

K. BEATRIX

In 2012 in Spain, paleontologists dug up what they believe to be fossil fragments of the upper and lower jaw and teeth of the oldest panda relative—they named the species *Kretzoiarctos beatrix*. They believe this small, tree-climbing, bear-like creature lived in the damp forests here about 12 million years ago. This extinct bear is the oldest recorded giant panda relative. Some scientists believe it might even be an ancestor of all bears (as opposed to an ancestor of the giant panda branch of the family), but no one knows for sure.

Like modern giant pandas. *K. beatrix* likely fed on tough plants and was an agile climber. Though *K. beatrix* was considerably smaller than today's giant pandas, probably weighing in at only about 130 pounds (60 kg), it had a lot more to worry about than its modern relatives. An extinct dog-like carnivore called the bear-dog inhabited the forests of southwestern Europe and likely hunted *K. beatrix*.

But fragments of 11-million-year-old bones can only tell us so much about the life of an extinct species. Scientists aren't really sure what happened to *K. beatrix* or precisely how the species fits in to bears' ancestry. But finding these fossils helped scientists put together an important piece of this very hairy bear-evolution puzzle.

GIANT PANDA (*Ailuropoda melanoleuca*)

PYGMY PANDA (*Ailuropoda microta*)

ANDEAN BEAR (*Tremarctos ornatus*)

3 million years ago *Ursus* began to diversify rapidly into many species.

ASIAN BLACK BEAR (*Ursus thibetanus*)

POLAR BEAR (*Ursus maritimus*)

BROWN BEAR (*Ursus arctos*)

AMERICAN BLACK BEAR (*Ursus americanus*)

URSUS MINIMUS

SLOTH BEAR (*Ursus ursinus*)

9 MIL   6 MIL   3 MIL

SUN BEAR (*Ursus malayanus*)

PANDA FILMMAKER

Nicolas Brown recalls the herd of 500 elk he used to see every day as a kid. They bedded down in front of his elementary school in the mountains of Colorado, U.S.A.

That field is now a housing development and the herd of elk is gone. Their disappearance has haunted him. It also influenced his career.

In the years since he admired the elk, Brown has zoomed in on his interest in wildlife conservation by filming powerful documentaries that tell the stories of animals. He became fascinated with pandas and their fight for survival.

Telling a story about giant pandas on location in China both challenged and amused Brown along the way. He had to work around mudslides and power outages for months while filming *Pandas: The Journey Home* (the movie features the panda Tao Tao, whom you read about on page 11). On the other hand, he laughed the day he witnessed an amazing adaptation of male giant pandas—they sometimes pee while doing a handstand. He learned that among male giant pandas, whoever can pee the highest up a tree is considered the strongest—even if the act involves a bit of acrobatics.

BUILT FOR BAMBOO

A panda's body has adapted to eating tough, fibrous bamboo. Check out some of these adaptations that have made bamboo its main menu item for millions of years.

A bone that acts like a thumb helps a panda grasp bamboo with great precision.

Powerful legs enable it to walk with ease through dense forest.

Today wildlife conservationists are working to restore wildlife corridors (connected stretches of protected panda habitat) between habitats so that smaller panda populations do not become permanently isolated and unable to reproduce.

Biologists refer to pandas having home ranges, which are simply the areas where they live. And they live where the food is. A newborn cub, about the size of a chipmunk, lives within the realm of its mother's warm body, feeding on the nutrition her milk provides. As it gets older, like a fifth grader allowed to walk to school with friends, a panda cub's world gets larger. Now it explores the bamboo patch where its mother sits and eats.

The size of an adult panda's home range depends on the resources the area holds. In general, an adult panda only needs as much space as the bamboo it takes to feed itself—about 30 pounds (14 kg) a day, give or take. In prime panda habitat a home range might be about two square miles (5 sq km). On a typical day, pandas don't travel much. They stay in a green patch of bamboo for a while and then move about 500 yards (457 m) to a different patch every so often.

>> EXPERT TIPS

Filmmaker Nicolas Brown's tips on how to make a panda video at the zoo:

1 Learn about the panda you're visiting and its original home, China.

2 Visit during feeding time, when pandas might be most active.

3 Appreciate the "Zen" footage of your video and pandas' calm lifestyle and be patient.

Wide, flat molars crush and grind the tough grass.

Its short muzzle and powerful jaws chomp thick stalks.

A furry rear end provides the perfect seat for dinner.

THE PEOPLE'S REPUBLIC OF CHINA

The Chinese government has had some big wins in the fight to save pandas in the recent past. Over the past two decades, the country's Department of Forestry has championed the cause, funding breeding centers and research.

China is working to save panda habitat, too. The country's Grain to Green program is focused on returning about 32 million acres (13 million ha) of farmland on steep mountainsides in the Shaanxi and Sichuan Provinces to a protected state. The project has helped restore habitat for pandas and also helped prevent flood disasters for people who live in the low-lying areas of the Yangtze and Yellow Rivers.

Other big wins for China when it comes to saving pandas and their environment include the country's limits on logging. The country has also created 64 protected panda reserves across southwestern China.

China also shares its pandas with other countries. China gifts, leases, or loans certain animals—like Bao Bao, whom you read about on page 20—to zoos around the world. Born in the United States, Bao Bao is scheduled to return to China when she turns four.

Pandas live solitary lives, in far-flung neighborhoods with other members of their species. Adult pandas usually stay away from one another except for the brief period each year when it's time to mate. Panda mothers and their cubs stick together for about two years.

FOUR SEASONS

Because they have to feed all year long (thanks to the low nutritional quality of bamboo), giant pandas don't hibernate. Instead they adjust to the seasons. In the snowy winter, pandas migrate, wandering down steep ravines to lower elevations to eat the most nutritious bamboo they can find.

In spring, pink primrose flowers bloom as the breeding season gets under way. When a female panda is nearly ready to mate, she begins to scent mark like crazy, allowing males to track her down. Then she begins to bleat and chirp. Males respond in the same way, disturbing the colorful birds that have returned after winter. A female might stay safe in a tree or on a high rock as the males congregate and compete—often engaging in violent fights—for the chance to mate with her.

In summer, giant pandas climb back up the mountains' slippery ravines to feed on tender new bamboo shoots. By August or September, a pregnant mother might find a den in the protection and shelter of the cavity (or a hole) at the base of an old tree in anticipation of a birth. Old trees make the best dens, but today, many of those old-growth forests are gone, due to decades of human destruction and logging. The mother-to-be may be forced to find shelter—however inadequate—in a cave or even settling for hiding in a bamboo thicket.

In autumn, mothers move around their home ranges more freely than when their cubs were newborn. Now, a mother teaches her cub to scamper up into a tree and wait while she "dines out."

LAND GRAB

Did you know that nearly one out of every seven people on this planet lives in China? There are 1.4 billion people in China out of more than 7 billion people on Earth. Human disturbances in the forest have created dangerous situations for pandas, like when bamboo is flowering. It's a naturally occurring reseeding process that—depending on the bamboo species—happens once every 10 to 100 years. But when it happens, entire patches of bamboo, or even areas of bamboo understory, are temporarily unavailable for eating (like when a vending machine goes out-of-order and needs to be restocked).

Even a hungry panda won't eat bamboo during the flowering stage. If flowering happened to just one plant, or one patch at a time, it would be no big deal. But all of the plants of the same species can reseed over a larger area at the same time. After it flowers, the plant drops a seed to the forest floor and dies. From a panda's point of view, the forest has gone from an all-you-can-eat smorgasbord to one closed-up café. And it can take five to seven years for new plants to be edible.

Throughout history, pandas have simply moved to "greener pastures" when bamboo flowers. There are different species of bamboo at different elevations. But because the giant pandas' range is limited to high elevation mountains, there are often only a few species available. Human expansion, involving roads, towns, mining operations, and mass agriculture, has knocked out massive amounts of bamboo forest. Now, when flowering occurs, pandas may not have the geographic flexibility to move to another area to find different species of bamboo that are not flowering. They're left without a food source, a deadly predicament for a giant panda.

FAST-GROWING BAMBOO IS ACTUALLY A TYPE OF GRASS WITH A WOODY STEM.

Light and dark shadows bounce through a dense bamboo forest in China, where pandas make their home in the wild.

HOWDY, NEIGHBOR!

Giant pandas live solitary lives, but they are far from alone. They live alongside other pandas, and also a variety of other diverse, and rare, wildlife.

The red panda shares the giant panda's high-altitude forest, but has a wider range that also includes Nepal and Myanmar (Burma).

Quick-footed mountain sheep like the Siberian ibex climb jagged slopes in giant panda territory and survive on sparse grass, twigs, and moss.

Golden eagles soar above the bamboo forest.

The endangered Sichuan golden snub-nosed monkey lives alongside giant pandas in the Wolong Nature Reserve in China.

The rare takin beats the cold with a nose that heats up the air before it reaches its lungs.

Endangered snow leopards survive in the same snowy mountains as giant pandas.

CHANGE IN CHINA

China is working hard to conserve its wild places. After thousands of years of human farming and hunting, giant pandas have become isolated, like tigers in Asia and Russia. If they can't find each other to mate, future generations of these hard-to-find animals won't exist. Imagine if your friends all lived far away and you had no way to reach them—no phones, texting, bicycles, school, or even snail mail.

Even in remote places, wild giant pandas face challenges—their habitat range is limited to high ridges and steep slopes, remote areas unsuitable for farming. Researchers track collared wild pandas, trying to understand how far they must go to find each other to breed. In 2014 scientists used a GPS system to track an unusual case in which a collared female panda had traveled more than 30 miles (48 km) in a day, likely trying to find a mate.

In protected areas like the Liziping Nature Reserve in Sichuan, China, where Tao Tao (from page 11) was released, there is wild space but there are so few pandas left that they have to work hard to find each other. The hope for Tao Tao is that he will find a mate and reproduce, helping repopulate the area.

The good news is that environmental and wildlife conservation is growing in China. The image of lovable, huggable pandas draws attention to conservation. The animal has come to symbolize hope for the environment—like when millions of people in China watched Tao Tao's release on live television and wished him good luck.

Logging impacts the natural landscape in Litang, located in China's Sichuan Province.

In China, farming villages and panda territory overlap.

Over the years giant pandas, as specialist eaters, evolved a taste for bamboo.

>>RESCUE ACTIVITIES

ACT

PUT ON A PANDA PUPPET SHOW

Pandas are captivating animals with interesting stories to tell. Put on a panda puppet show and help raise awareness of panda life, habits, and current conservation efforts.

MAKE

RAISE FUNDS THROUGH A PANDA PUPPET SHOW.

COMMISSION WWF TO LIST SAFE-AWAY-AS-A PANDA PROGRAM to hand out at your puppet show. The more tickets you sell, the more money goes toward saving pandas.

PICK A GREAT PLACE TO PROMOTE Get your parent or guardian's permission before you start marketing your show.

PICK YOUR PRICE CAREFULLY Decide if you are raising money and need to make a profit, or if you are happy to simply give the tickets away.

CREATE PANDA PUPPETS.

SOCK PUPPETS ARE SIMPLE AND GREAT FOR SHOWING EXPRESSIONS You could use a needle and thread to sew black and white socks together, along with a couple of buttons.

GOT SOME WHITE PAPER PLATES? Use scissors and glue to make a giant panda puppet. With enough plates you could make a life-size puppet.

SHADOW PUPPETS ARE HARD TO MASTER but they are an inexpensive way to make a puppet. Shine a beam of light onto your hands and see if you can make a puppet on a wall. This is very tricky, so good luck!

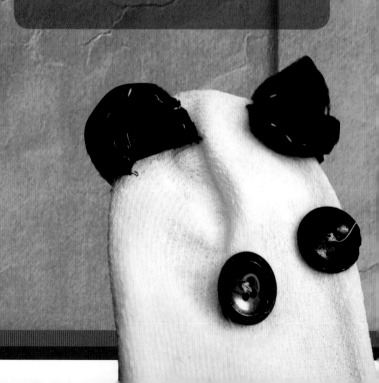

SHARE

RAISE AWARENESS.

You can explain that pandas are specialist animals that are awesome at eating bamboo but not much else.

and restore wild places so they can thrive. You could include some of this information in your show or in the program you hand out to attendees.

They could sign a petition, give you a donation that can be passed to a panda charity, or help in another way.

Putting on a good puppet show is not easy. Here are some tips to make your show a success:

1 Make sure you have a good story line. Picking a story true to life is a great way to make your performance memorable and authentic.

2 Create a script with stage directions based on the story. This should include what will be said and who needs to do what.

3 Have fun. The more you enjoy yourself, the better your panda puppet performance will be.

CHAPTER 3

>> PANDA FAMILY

A mother playfully bonds with her cub.

"IN ITS OWN REALM, A PANDA APPEARS NEITHER CUDDLY NOR CLUMSY, BUT AN IMPOSING AND POWERFUL VISION OF BEAUTY."

—GEORGE SCHALLER, INTERNATIONAL WILDLIFE CONSERVATIONIST

To call its mother, a panda cub, like this captive panda in China, might make a loud squawk.

T
he bond between a mother giant panda and her cub—captive or wild—is one of the most important relationships among pandas. Like in human families, a mother has a lot of jobs. She provides food for her young, protects them, teaches them, snuggles them, and disciplines them. A giant panda mother does that too.

MOM IN CHARGE

Elusive and shy, giant pandas are hard to observe in the wild. Researchers track wild pandas with help from data provided by radio telemetry and GPS. They watch video downloaded from motion-detecting camera traps set up in the wild (some right inside mothers' dens). These informational bread crumbs provide a few details of wild pandas' family life.

If she has a cub that survives, it will be two years before Mama Bear can get pregnant again. Her pregnancy usually averages about five months, but it varies widely, due to a survival adaptation specific to bears. If conditions aren't right (like if there isn't available food or if the mother is in poor health) a pregnant female panda's body will slow down or end the development process going on inside the womb.

Between March and July, a pregnant panda will eat bamboo shoots progressively from low to high altitudes. She'll consume important nutrition and gain about 40 pounds (18 kg) along the way—another reason why the forest is so important to the success of efforts to save giant pandas.

As a giant panda mom prepares to deliver, instinct tells her to find a safe place to den. This temporary spot will protect her and her fragile offspring until the cub is big enough to venture outside.

Newborn cubs are helpless, blind, and pink. A panda mother delivers twins

A RECENT STUDY SHOWED THAT A MOTHER PANDA CAN RECOGNIZE THE SCENT OF HER CUB, EVEN AFTER YEARS OF NOT SEEING EACH OTHER.

about half the time, but in the wild, only one survives. At birth, a cub weighs only about 3.5 ounces (99 g)— about the same weight as a king-size candy bar. A giant panda mom weighs about 900 times more than her tiny cub. If the same were true about humans, your mom would have to have weighed about as much as 24 NFL football players when you were born.

Despite her size, a panda mother is very gentle. She uses her mouth to put the cub down next to her before slowly lying down, picking it up, and resting it on her belly to nurse. A small cub snuggles into its mom's belly fur, rising and falling with her breath. The baby's survival depends on its mother's ability to provide protection from cold, parasites, and predators. While adult pandas don't have any predators, cubs are vulnerable to the yellow-throated marten, the golden cat, and an occasional leopard that shares its forest.

A mother bear provides food and constant care. She won't eat, drink, or even relieve herself for days because she must hold her cub to keep it warm. Imagine your mom not eating, drinking, or going to the bathroom for days because it wasn't safe to put her baby down!

PANDA CUB TIME LINE

A baby panda looks something like a tooth-less, naked mole rat when it's born, and weighs about the same as an iPhone. But things change quickly:

After a week, a cub's pink skin begins to turn black where black fur will grow—first the eye patches, then the ears, shoulders, and legs.

By three weeks old, a cub is covered in black and white fur and weighs more than a pound (.45 kg).

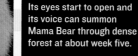

Its eyes start to open and its voice can summon Mama Bear through dense forest at about week five.

At about 12 weeks old, a cub starts learning to crawl by scooting and pushing its legs underneath its body.

At six months old, a cub might start climbing trees, figuring out which branches will hold him and which ones will snap and send him tumbling.

By its first birthday, a cub might weigh 50 or 60 pounds (23 or 27 kg).

PAN PAN

When prime bamboo forests in panda habitats died off as part of the natural bamboo reseeding process called flowering (remember reading about this in Chapter 2?), about 130 endangered wild pandas starved to death in the mid-1970s. They didn't have enough backup bamboo, thanks to human expansion. When another flowering episode occurred in 1986, panda rescue teams searched the forest to save starving pandas. In the mountains of Baoxing, one team found a lethargic, very thin, two-month-old orphan cub.

A panda researcher carried the cub out of the forest, named him Pan Pan (meaning "hope"), and rehabilitated him along with another cub. The two male cubs wrestled, played, and ate in the researcher's one-room home. At night, the three slept together on a narrow bed.

In the early 1990s, bright-eyed Pan Pan arrived at the Wolong Panda Center in China. Over the years, he has become the world's most successful captive panda sire. Today, at age 30, he has more cubs, grand-cubs, and great grand-cubs (a total of 32, 16 of which are still living) than any other panda alive today.

These days, Pan Pan lives a comfortable life at the Dujiangyan Giant Panda Rescue and Disease Control Center, a panda rescue and treatment center.

PANDA SCHOOL

In the wild, a panda mom teaches her cub all it will need to know to survive. She teaches it lessons about food, like what to eat and where to find it. Even though the cub won't eat bamboo until it has adult teeth, even before it starts to walk, a cub will sit with its mother and nosh on a leaf here or there just for fun while she eats. Chewing and playing with mom's bamboo is a critical introduction to the food it will eat for the rest of its life. The cub will also learn how good an occasional rodent tastes and how to find a stream and break through the ice, depending on the season, for a drink.

The mother also teaches her cub a lot simply by reacting to things that she comes across, like other pandas or a leopard. The cub observes and learns like a star student.

When the cub's first birthday nears at the end of the summer, it might weigh 50 or 60 pounds (23 or 27 kg) and is on the verge of having a full-time job: stuffing its face with crunchy bamboo for hours every day. Around its second birthday, Mama Bear encourages her cub to move on to a more independent life. It's like when a kid grows up and no longer needs to live at home.

>> ANIMAL RESCUE!

WOLONG GIANT PANDA BREEDING CENTER

In 2008 a major earthquake rocked China. The ground shuddered and shook around the giant pandas and their caregivers at the Wolong Giant Panda Breeding Center in Sichuan, the world's largest giant panda breeding and research facility and home to 60 pandas. In two minutes of terror, entire mountainsides sheared off, destroying the breeding center, the surrounding bamboo forests, villages, and schools.

At the center, keepers ran to the enclosures to save pandas. Many were saved, like Guo Guo (you'll read about her and the earthquake on page 85), but some were not so lucky. A wonderful mother panda named Mao Mao was missing—no one knew if she had escaped or was crushed under an enclosure wall in the wreckage. The breeding center was in shambles. The surviving pandas were taken to a temporary location. Three weeks after the earthquake, Mao Mao's keepers found her body. The next morning, they held a funeral to celebrate her life.

In the years that have followed, the damaged facility (now referred to as Hetaoping) has been used for the rewilding program. The facility is in the Wolong Nature Reserve (similar to a national park), which covers 494,210 acres (200,000 ha) of the pristine wilderness area that is home to many species of animals. Its mountains rise to elevations of up to 20,500 feet (6,248 m). The reserve was established in 1963 to further the Chinese government's commitment to preserve the giant panda.

In some ways, the earthquake has helped pandas and the conservationists trying to save the species. Few tourists visit. As the area has returned to a more wild state, the pandas have thrived.

A bigger breeding center has been built in nearby Gengda. Rebuilding the center has been a crucial milestone to the giant panda's survival as a species.

DR. SARAH BEXELL

BORN: MINNESOTA, U.S.A.
JOB TITLE: DIRECTOR OF CONSERVATION EDUCATION AT THE CHENGDU RESEARCH BASE OF GIANT PANDA BREEDING AND UNIVERSITY OF DENVER
LOCATION: CHINA AND U.S.A.
YEARS WORKING WITH PANDAS: 15

How are you helping to save pandas?

Our conservation education department runs many educational programs for all ages. We mostly teach local students in Chengdu, the capital of Sichuan Province, where the majority of wild giant pandas still live. We also train teachers and nature reserve staff to run their own conservation education programs. I hope our efforts will help save space for all the other amazing beings, beautiful plants, and ecosystem in southwestern China.

What's your favorite thing about your job?

Working with children who care and want to protect animals of any species.

What's the best thing about working in the field?

Knowing what is really happening to animals and wild places.

What's the worst thing about working in the field?

Sometimes, it feels more and more hopeless every single day, but finding people who care and want to help animals and the Earth keeps me motivated.

How can kids prepare to do your job one day?

Learn all you can! Study hard and ask hard questions. It doesn't matter what field you choose to study, do your best at whatever makes you happy—art, law, science, drama, sports, anything, and use it to support saving animals and nature.

Observing a cub named Shi Shi and recording his development. His love and trust in his mom, Cheng Cheng, and her devoted love and care for him cemented my knowledge of their beautiful minds, emotions, and bonds with each other.

A baby panda leans on its mother.

A panda mother in the wild nuzzles her cub just outside the den.

NOSE-TO-TAIL COMMUNICATION

Since a panda can't text or IM other pandas about its whereabouts or when it will be home, it relies on smell as its number one communication tool. It's a three-dimensional world of odors, almost impossible for a human to comprehend.

A newborn cub quickly learns its mother's smell. It's a critical connection. And as it gets older, that "sniff channel" gives a panda the important ability to receive messages and learn about its environment through smell. And it can leave a trail of scents through urine and secretions with help from the many scent glands on its body.

Through the perfumed scents it leaves, a panda posts updates about its identity, age, and sex. The scents are even somehow "time-stamped" so other pandas know when the scent message was left.

The giant panda's furry white tail plays a big role in the business of communication. The giant panda does not wag or twitch its tail to communicate like a dog or a

>> PANDA SPOTLIGHT

CHOW TIME
Giant pandas spend hours a day eating.

When it comes to bamboo, a panda eats the leaves first, ripping them off the stalks and wadding the leaves up before eating them.

Before eating a bamboo stalk, a panda uses its teeth to strip off the plastic-like outer layer.

ANIMAL SUPERPOWERS

PANDA CUB WORKOUT

BABY PANDAS WORK OUT EVERY DAY TO BUILD MUSCLES AND IMPROVE THEIR COORDINATION.

THEY WRIGGLE AND ROLL THEMSELVES ALONG FOR SHORT DISTANCES.

AT TWO MONTHS OLD, THEY HAVE THEIR OWN DAILY PANDA CUB WORKOUT: PUSH! STRETCH! KICK!

THEY DO "CRUNCHES" TO TURN BABY FAT INTO HARD MUSCLE.

Zoo pandas also nibble "panda bread" as well as sugarcane, high-fiber biscuits, carrots, apples, and sweet potatoes.

Handlers in wild training programs deliver food while wearing panda suits so the pandas don't see or smell the humans.

LIKE ALL BEARS, WHEN A PANDA CLIMBS DOWN A TREE, HE GOES RUMP FIRST.

Captive-bred Cao Cao teaches her panda cub how to climb at China's Wolong Panda Center's wild training base.

cat. Unless a panda is busy spreading scents, its tail stays tucked close to its body. But when it wants to send a message, a panda uses its tail to smear odor from a large scent gland under the tail on any surface it might pass. That smell sends out a signal, kind of like a GPS system. Other pandas pick up on the signal and get the message—whether it's "I'm ready to mate" or "keep out." A male panda can smell a female ready to mate from about 18 miles (29 km) away.

A panda also spreads messages by transmitting smells with help from its ears. Using its big paws, a panda wipes smelly secretions on its ears. They act like megaphones broadcasting the scent on to the wind.

Biologists take everything they know about how these wonderful animals live and use the information to help save the species. Survival rates of cubs and what scientists call recruitment, or how many cubs live to reproduce, is vital information for conservationists to understand what's happening in a panda population. The good news is that those numbers are rising in captivity. Numbers are hard to come by in the wild, but the science indicates that the wild populations are stable and even increasing.

A mother and her cub love to play, snuggle, and relax together.

SCENT PAINTING

It stinks that pandas have lost homes and are endangered. This challenge is the perfect way to give people the message that pandas and other wildlife need protecting. Pandas use their tails to make scent messages that can be smelled from 18 miles (29 km) away. How far can you spread your message and raise awareness for pandas?

A young panda spreads its scent message on a tree.

MAKE

PAINT SMELLY PANDAS.

COLLECT SOME SMELLY, EDIBLE, AND CLEAR LIQUIDS.
Vanilla, mint, and almond are all good scents to choose. Give each of the scents a different meaning. Vanilla could mean "love," while almond might translate to "fear."

MAKE A SCENT PAINTING USING REGULAR PAINT. You could paint a panda, a panda's home, or the habitat they have lost. Try painting with regular paint, letting it dry, and then adding your scent over the top.

PAINT NEW SMELLY ART BY USING THE LIQUIDS YOU COLLECTED EARLIER. You could paint a map that reveals how much habitat pandas have lost, but the only way to get the message is by having a sniff.

ACT

HOLD AN ART EXHIBITION.

TAKE ACTION AND HOLD AN EXHIBITION OF YOUR SMELLY PANDA ART. Pick a place where lots of people will be able to see—and smell—your work.

MAKE SURE YOUR AUDIENCE GETS THE MESSAGE BY CREATING AN INFORMATION BOARD. This board should include information about who you are, why you are holding the exhibition, and how they can help you help pandas.

INVOLVE PEOPLE BY PROVIDING SCENTS, PAINTS, AND PAPER for them to make their own panda paintings. Can you paint 1,900 pandas? This is the estimate of how many are left in the wild.

Here are some good tips on how to hold a smelly exhibition:

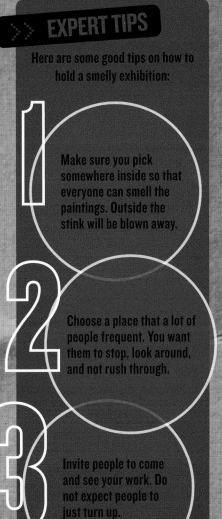

1 Make sure you pick somewhere inside so that everyone can smell the paintings. Outside the stink will be blown away.

2 Choose a place that a lot of people frequent. You want them to stop, look around, and not rush through.

3 Invite people to come and see your work. Do not expect people to just turn up.

SHARE

MAKE A STINK.

You may not be able to make your actual scent travel for miles, like a panda, but you can make your message go even farther.

Ask them to share the photos with their friends and family, or with a wildlife organization such as **NG Kids'** photo community, **MyShot.** Online they could also include a hashtag like **#ProtectPandas** or **#NGMissionPandaRescue.**

Tell them about your exhibition and ask the audience to show support for your campaign by giving a donation or signing a petition.

"THROUGH THE ECOLOGICAL RESTORATION OF PANDA HABITAT, WE CAN CHART A NEW COURSE."

— MARC BRODY, FOUNDER AND PRESIDENT, PANDA MOUNTAIN

CHAPTER 4

LEARNING FROM PANDAS

Today pandas struggle to survive, but conservationists hope to rewild them to their natural habitats.

An hour after she gives birth to her first cub, a giant panda named Ya Ya cradles her newborn to her chest. She licks him clean in a denning enclosure at the Chengdu Research Base of Giant Panda Breeding in China's Sichuan Province.

A MOTHER'S TOUCH

Graduate student Rebecca Snyder sits on a bamboo stool outside the nursery house. She marvels at Ya Ya's dedication and her gentle touch despite the size difference between mom and baby. As a student, Snyder observes for about nine hours a day. She takes notes, fills out data sheets, and refers to a behavior catalog called an ethogram. It's a quiet, relaxing job. She watches, listens, and jots down what she sees, even while the pandas sleep.

STUDYING GIANT PANDAS

For more than two years in China, Snyder's job was to study the behavior of giant pandas living in zoos and breeding centers to better understand what pandas need to mate, raise their cubs, and live long, healthy lives. Today, in her job as coordinator of the Giant Panda Program for Zoo Atlanta in Georgia, U.S.A., she has a very special opportunity to both manage the care of animals and do research. Many biologists in her field only get the chance to do one or the other.

Ya Ya and her cub, who will later be named Yang Yang, are some of the first pandas in Snyder's study. Ya Ya's mother and grandmother were some of the best mothers at Chengdu. The staff refers to them as "hero mothers" because they have raised so many healthy cubs.

AT FIVE YEARS OLD, A FEMALE PANDA IS READY TO HAVE CUBS OF HER OWN.

A captive panda named Yang Yang takes a time-out from playing and enjoys a bamboo snack at Zoo Atlanta in the U.S.A.

Yang Yang naps on a log in his enclosure at Zoo Atlanta.

PANDA KINDERGARTEN

Pandas at the Bifengxia Panda Base in China go to kindergarten, like human children do.

At school, they take naps at naptime.

They have recess—playing tag, racing down the slide, climbing rocks, doing somersaults, and swinging on tire swings.

They use their keepers as jungle gyms.

Sometimes they fall down, like this panda that fell off a rocking horse.

They snack on bamboo cakes made from ground bamboo, soybeans, corn, rice, eggs, sugar, and salt.

They get tired and take breaks in trees.

Snyder enjoys the quiet time with pandas. She loves getting to know each one individually and learning to understand what they do. Her research has increased conservationists' understanding of the relationship between mothers and cubs. One lesson Snyder learned is how important it is for cubs to remain with their mothers until they are old enough to live on their own, even in zoos.

When Yang Yang is two, he leaves his home in China to join the panda family at Zoo Atlanta. There, Snyder spends about five hours a week observing the pandas as part of her job as curator of mammals. Yang Yang (his name means "little sea") will always have a special place in Snyder's heart, since she met him when he was just an hour old. She describes him as a bit of a goofball—very curious, active, and good at climbing as a cub. Today, here in the United States, Yang Yang teaches thousands of visitors about the life of pandas. He has fathered five cubs, including the twins Mei Lun and Mei Huan that you read about on page 21.

>> EXPERT TIPS

Wolong Panda Center's Zhang Hemin's tips for how kids can help save pandas:

1 Talk to your parents about making a trip to visit and volunteer at the China Conservation and Research Center for the Giant Panda in China.

2 Pay attention to giant panda–related information, new discoveries, and news about the birth of panda cubs.

3 Share what you learn about panda conservation with your friends and classmates.

>> ANIMAL RESCUE!

OUCH! LESSON LEARNED

Pandas might look as cuddly as stuffed animals, but their big white teeth, powerful jaws, and sharp claws are nothing to toy with. These roly-poly bears can pack a punch, like the day Wolong Panda Center's Zhang Hemin tried to teach a one-year-old panda cub how to climb a tree.

Zhang has developed training programs to help small wild panda populations grow and to reintroduce pandas to places where they are no longer found. But figuring out how to "rewild" captive-born pandas isn't easy. The pandas must learn how to navigate the challenges of wild living. The people must learn how to teach, and when to step back and let another panda do the teaching.

That day in 1997, Zhang repeatedly lifted the cub and put it on a low branch. After an hour, the panda bit him on the lower leg. A keeper pried the panda's jaws off of Zhang's calf, but it took months in the hospital for Zhang to recover.

Later, he watched a panda mom teach her cub to climb a tree with remarkable ease. First she demonstrated, then

used her head to push the little one into the tree. If the cub got too high she pulled him down with her teeth or by the scruff of the cub's neck.

Zhang realized that panda mothers are much better qualified than humans to teach panda cubs how to climb trees. Lesson learned!

Back in China, Ya Ya keeps up the good work, giving birth to 13 cubs throughout her reproductive years. In addition to helping teach humans about pandas, Ya Ya is one of the best panda moms in the world, helping repopulate the species and teaching her cubs well. Today she's retired and living at the Chengdu Zoo as one of its famous pandas on exhibit.

SAVING A SPECIES

Each new panda born is a cause for celebration. Wolong Panda Center director Zhang Hemin is known around the world as Papa Panda. He has dedicated the last 30 years of his life to saving pandas from extinction by figuring out how to get pandas to successfully mate in captivity and how to keep the cubs alive once they're born. By training pandas and releasing them back into the wild, he hopes to rejuvenate small wild populations of pandas and also to reintroduce pandas to areas where pandas used to live wild.

Breeding pandas in captivity can be difficult. Female pandas are fertile for only about two days a year. The animals have to have enough scent exposure to each other to know when it's the right time for mating. In zoos, researchers experiment with how to get the timing just right. They do things like have male and female pandas swap enclosures so they can get the scent messages left by other pandas to increase the chance of a pregnancy.

TRADING PLACES

Another technique that human caregivers employ to help cubs survive in captivity is called swapping. In the wild, panda mothers have twins about half the time. When twins are born, panda moms have a hard time taking care of two cubs, and one usually dies. But in captivity, both cubs have the chance to survive and thrive with help from human care.

When conservationists first started breeding giant pandas in captivity, only about a third of cubs born in captivity survived. Zhang and his team studied mother pandas and how they raised their cubs to learn how to help panda cubs thrive in captivity. They developed the system of care called swapping.

Baby swaps mean around-the-clock work for zoo nursery keepers. They rotate the cubs between the

(continued on page 72)

IN CHINESE, THE PHRASE *WO LONG* MEANS "SLEEPING DRAGON."

MENG MENG, SHUAI SHUAI, AND KUKU

The triplet panda cubs born early one morning at the Chimelong Safari Park in Guangzhou, China, in July 2014 are the only set of surviving triplets on record. They were born to mom Ju Xiao within four hours of each other.

One month after their birth, the panda cubs—one female and two males—have grown their black eye patches and black hair on their ears. By four months old, they had each grown two small white teeth perfect for ripping apart their mom's bamboo leaves.

These days, the cubs enjoy climbing rocks in their outdoor enclosure, wrestling with each other, tackling bamboo stalks, and playing peek-a-boo.

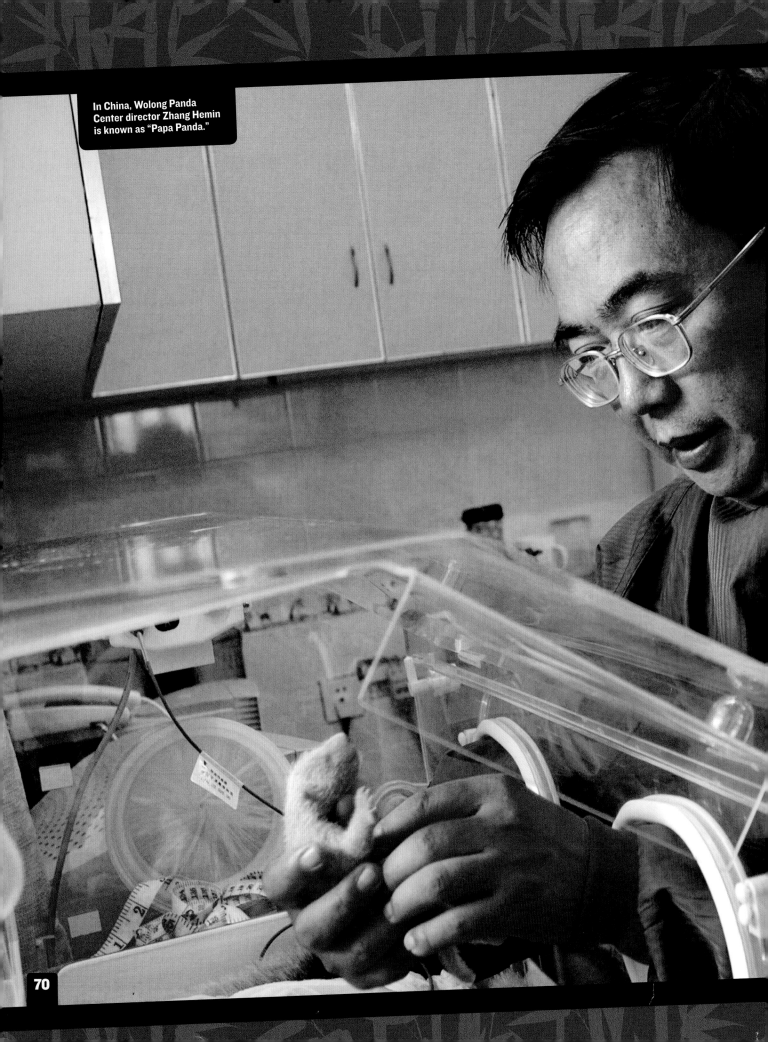

>> EXPLORER INTERVIEW

ZHANG HEMIN

BORN: YINGSHAN COUNTY, SICHUAN PROVINCE, CHINA
JOB TITLE: DIRECTOR OF CHINA CONSERVATION AND RESEARCH CENTER FOR THE GIANT PANDA AND DIRECTOR OF WOLONG NATURE RESERVE ADMINISTRATION
LOCATION: CHINA
YEARS WORKING WITH PANDAS: 32
MONTHS A YEAR IN THE FIELD: 12

How are you helping to save pandas?
By leading breeding research, increasing species population, and releasing pandas back into the wild after they get rewilding training.

What's your favorite thing about your job?
Playing and living with pandas.

What's the best thing about working in the field?
Working to establish giant panda conservation zones. To date, China has built 64 giant panda conservation zones.

What's the worst thing about working in the field?
Discovering poachers and foot clamps set to catch and kill pandas during patrol work. Sometimes pandas might get injured.

How can kids prepare to do your job one day?
They need three things: a strong, healthy body that can endure hardship and can climb, a basic knowledge of biology, and a loving heart.

>> MEMORABLE MOMENT

Hearing the sharp cry of a newborn panda, one summer day at the breeding center at Hetaoping base in China. A panda named Ying Ying had given birth to twins—making history as the first successful breeding via artificial insemination. We had waited and worried for days. When the babies finally arrived, I thought our sudden cheers from the monitoring room would blow off the roof.

Newborn giant panda cubs snuggle and stay warm in an incubator while they wait for their next meal.

mom and the keepers so each cub gets constant care and critical time with its mother. The system is like panda intensive care and helps increase each cub's chance for survival.

The panda mom you read about earlier in the chapter, Ya Ya, and her brother were the first twins to ever survive in captivity, thanks to swapping. When Lun Lun the giant panda gave birth to twin cubs in July 2013 at Zoo Atlanta in Georgia, U.S.A., both of her cubs had a chance to survive and contribute to the panda population because of this technique.

In addition to providing extra food and warmth to the cubs, swapping enables the keepers to keep a close eye on the cubs' weight, temperature, and condition. This process also helps the keepers get to know the cubs. Lun Lun's first cub ("Cub A") was short and chubby and known around the nursery for being a fussy fuzz ball. If she got cold or hungry, she squealed and whined the way a human baby might cry. "Cub B" was slightly longer and slimmer when she was a tiny cub. She was also squirmier, and sometimes Lun Lun had a hard time getting her to settle down to sleep.

Nursery keepers rotated the cubs between Lun Lun and a warm incubator every few hours for months after

>> PANDA SPOTLIGHT

PANDA PAD

Zoos go to extremes to set up perfect panda enclosures that mimic life in the wild.

Pandas scamper up climbing structures, fallen logs, and rocks.

Live trees provide shade so pandas don't overheat.

PANDA KEEPER

For giant panda keeper Ming Wei (魏明 in written Chinese), feeding baby pandas is like feeding his own children. He carries the cubs he takes care of in his hands when they are tiny and watches them grow bigger day by day. Ming works and lives at the China Conservation and Research Center for the Giant Panda in the Wolong Nature Reserve in China's Sichuan Province.

His job is simple: help the baby pandas grow up healthy and happy. Each morning he checks the panda cubs to see if they had a good night's sleep. He keeps their enclosure clean and prepares their food. He watches them eat and makes notes about what they do. He says watching the funny faces they make is his favorite part of the day. He loves seeing a baby panda he's cared for all grown up, especially when they have babies of their own.

Ming is helping save pandas by raising them when their mothers can't, like raising the twins that wouldn't have survived without human intervention. Ming is like a Mr. Mom to the panda cubs. He watches over them like their own mother would.

Cooled grottoes (caves) provide privacy for naps.

A mist machine and a bamboo patch make the enclosure feel like home.

Splash! It's fun to cool off and play in the water.

PANDAS HAVE A LIFE SPAN OF ABOUT 14 YEARS IN THE WILD AND MORE THAN 30 YEARS IN CAPTIVITY.

Despite slippery snow, a wild cub in China's Wolong Nature Reserve climbs up a tree.

their birth. It took a while to get her to accept swapping, but after the first few tries, the giant panda seemed to understand that her trusted keepers were helping. She also knew that by coming to the edge of her enclosure to let the keepers take one baby and return the other, she'd get a stalk of sweet, crunchy sugarcane.

When the cubs reached their 100th day of life, Zoo Atlanta announced their names according to Chinese tradition. The names—Mei Lun and Mei Huan—were based on a Chinese phrase that means "indescribably beautiful and magnificent."

By this time, the cubs no longer needed to be swapped; they stayed with their mother full-time, getting cuter by the day. They also explored—playing, climbing, and investigating their environment—inspiring zoo visitors to help save giant pandas. As the first twin cubs to survive in the United States due to swapping, they give hope for the future of this endangered species.

MILESTONES

Scientists work hard to learn how to care for pandas in captivity. As a result, the survival rate for cubs born in captivity has skyrocketed from about 30 percent two decades ago to about 95 percent today.

Breeding centers in China and zoos around the world now successfully deliver between 30 and 40 bouncing baby panda cubs into the arms of panda moms every year. In 2013, the number of giant pandas living in zoos and breeding facilities around the world grew to nearly 400.

Most of the captive-born babies—because they've been around humans their entire lives and lack survival skills—will either stay at their homes in China and breed or travel overseas to live in approved zoos.

Mei Lun and Mei Huan spend time in their nursery box before one of them is removed to stay with Lun Lun as part of the swapping process.

>> RESCUE ACTIVITIES

BE A WILDLIFE PHOTOGRAPHER

Photography is a good way to study, enjoy, and even protect wildlife. Depending on where you live, you may not be able to photograph wild pandas, but you can practice all the same skills. Before traveling to distant places, most National Geographic photographers learned to take great pictures in their own communities. Do this challenge to improve your photographic skills.

ACT

BIOBLITZ A PLACE.

A BioBlitz is an attempt to record all the living species within an area. You could do this in your garden, a local park, or somewhere else.

ORGANIZE A GROUP OF FRIENDS AND FAMILY TO PARTICIPATE WITH YOU. The more eyes you have counting, the more species you will be able to record.

YOU COULD INVITE AN EXPERT ALONG TO HELP YOU. They will be able to find and identify things that you may not recognize.

MAKE

PRACTICE YOUR SKILLS.

PACK A CAMERA, SOME LUNCH AND WATER, AND WEAR THE RIGHT CLOTHES so that you are comfortable. Decide on a good place to see wildlife and take yourself on an adventure to see what you can find there.

PRACTICE YOUR SKILLS AS A PHOTOGRAPHER BY TAKING DIFFERENT KINDS OF PICTURES. Try to get as close as you can to an insect, without the photograph going out of focus. Slowly take pictures of bigger things.

HIDE SOMEWHERE AND BE VERY QUIET. See if you can get a photograph of an elusive animal that normally stays away from people. Remember to keep your distance and stay out of sight, so you don't disturb the animal in its home.

SHARE WHAT YOU FIND.

TELL YOUR PARENT, GRANDPARENT, OR TEACHER about what you find and ask them to look at your photos.

PHOTOGRAPHS CAN TELL A LOT OF STORIES. If you upload your photographs to Project Noah, iNaturalist, or National Geographic's Great Nature Project at www.greatnatureproject.org, you can get help to identify what you have photographed or contribute to a cool citizen science program.

ORGANIZE YOUR PHOTOS IN AN ALBUM so the design tells a story about panda life. Share your photos and unlock trophies on National Geographic Kids My Shot website at kids-myshot.nationalgeographic.com.

Use these tips to take a great photo:

1 Look through magazines and see what photos look good to you. What is it about the composition of the photo that you like or dislike? Research photo tips or ask someone who is good with cameras.

2 Play around with all of your camera's settings. Try changing a setting, taking a photo, and seeing how it changes. The more you play, the more you will learn.

3 Try to get a different perspective by taking pictures from lots of different angles, such as very low to the ground, or high up on a hill.

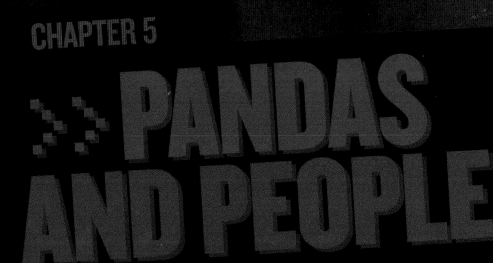

CHAPTER 5

PANDAS AND PEOPLE

"KIDS HAVE THE POWER TO INSPIRE AWARENESS, CARING, AND ACTION IN OTHERS TO HELP SAVE GIANT PANDAS."

— REBECCA SNYDER, ZOO ATLANTA GIANT PANDA PROGRAM COORDINATOR

A three-week-old panda cub gets around-the-clock care from keepers at China Conservation and Research Center for the Giant Panda in Bifengxia.

oday the giant panda is the national symbol of China. The panda has been a subject of fascination in Chinese literature, geography, and medicine books for thousands of years. Some scientists say prehistoric humans may have eaten pandas, but even though people in modern-day China consume parts and products from many wild animals—from shark fins to bear bile—you won't find giant panda on the menu.

PANDAS THROUGHOUT HISTORY

The earliest records of people and pandas may have involved fear of the unusual animals, which would lumber out of the forest on rare occasions to raid villages and lick cooking implements made out of iron or copper. Some scientists chalk these stories up to mere folklore.

Later in the history of Chinese culture, mind-sets changed. The panda was thought to have protective powers. During the Ming dynasty, people believed that a panda's pelt could keep away illness. In other ancient Chinese cultures, sleeping on a panda pelt was said to prevent the growth of tumors. A panda skull found in a royal tomb, dating from 179 to 163 B.C., suggests that the animal was held in high esteem.

Westerners first learned about giant pandas in 1869 when a French missionary named Armand David, also known as Père David, delivered the pelt of a wild panda to the National Museum of Natural History in Paris, France. The museum presented the giant panda as a new species the following year. Today, the animal is thought to have inspired the contrasting black and white Chinese yin and yang symbol, an ancient symbol representing the opposing forces of the universe, like life and death.

PANDAS, NOT PETS

The giant panda reached iconic status in the United States in the 1930s when a socialite named Ruth Harkness traveled to China and hired a guide to take her into the mountains and find her a panda cub she could take home. The cub would be a tribute to her late explorer husband.

Two young pandas wrestle on a log, building strength and agility.

PANDAS HAVE BEEN REFERENCED IN CHINESE LITERATURE FOR AT LEAST 2,000 YEARS.

After three days of searching, the guide's team found a cub. It's possible that they had to kill the mother panda to capture the baby. Harkness carried a male cub out of the forest in a blanket, named him Su Lin, and fed him powdered milk from a baby bottle. To smuggle him out of the country, she claimed the cub was a dog.

Back in the United States, Su Lin lived in Harkness's New York apartment. He was later sold to Chicago's Brookfield Zoo, where he died before his second birthday. Today, you can visit Su Lin's body, where it's on display at the Field Museum of Natural History in Chicago, Illinois.

So what are the lessons learned from Su Lin's story? At the time of his capture, his story was not unique—many zoo animals during that time were acquired from the wild and caregivers, tragically, knew little about how to care for them. The good news is that modern zoos have come a long way. Most zoos get animals from other zoos and have highly qualified caregivers. Many zoos, like those accredited by the Association of Zoos and Aquariums, contribute to, or in some cases drive, the conservation of wild populations.

According to the International Union for Conservation of Nature, the problem of poaching (the illegal killing or capturing of animals, like baby Su Lin) was a serious problem in the past, but isn't considered a major threat for pandas today. Unlike some endangered animals, such as tigers, rhinoceroses, and elephants, panda body parts are not used in traditional Asian medicine. But poaching giant pandas does still happen.

In 1988, 203 people were arrested in China's Sichuan Province in connection with 146 recovered panda pelts—this represented a whopping one of every seven pandas thought to be alive at the time. In 2001, three men were arrested for trying to sell a panda pelt to an undercover police officer for $93,000 (an illegal leopard skin might cost $300,000 or an illegal tiger skin could cost $124,000).

Today, the penalties for poaching a giant panda (like life in prison) exceed the market value. Sadly, wild pandas are still sometimes killed in snares set for deer or other animals in the forest.

ANIMAL RESCUE!

FUGUI WAN A LOCAL PANDA PROTECTOR

The U.S.-based organization Panda Mountain works to conserve and restore giant panda habitat, in part by training both nature reserve personnel and local residents in the Wolong Nature Reserve, and other protected lands in the Sichuan Province. Fugui Wan serves as a coordinator for this work.

Wan lives in Wolong in a rural village. Working for Panda Mountain, he helps local villagers continue their farming lifestyle and improve their standard of living by creating native plant nurseries on the villager's farm land. By growing native plants and trees, which will be transplanted into nearby forests to restore panda habitat, these farmers establish a way to live green and reduce livestock grazing that degrades Wolong's mountain ecosystems.

Serving as a connection between scientists, conservationists, and his neighbors has made him grateful for both sides—he loves learning about pandas and helping save the bamboo forest. But he's also discovered a new pride for his misty mountain home. Once on a four-day hike from Four Sisters Mountain National Park into the Wolong Nature Reserve to survey the area, Wan stood on a mountaintop in the middle of a big cloud. He couldn't see very far and didn't realize he had walked into the middle of a herd of about 300 wild mountain sheep.

He loves to share stories with his neighbors and talk about how lucky they all are to live in such a special place—and the importance of protecting it.

PANDAS IN CULTURE

For thousands of years, humans have admired the giant panda with great enthusiasm.

At the 2008 Olympic Games in Beijing, China, a panda mascot represented the forest.

The panda has been celebrated on coins, like this one-ounce gold coin, throughout Chinese history.

Giant pandas may have inspired the Chinese symbol for yin and yang, which represents opposing forces of the universe, such as life and death.

Ancient Chinese cultures believed that sleeping on panda fur could ward off ghosts.

An animated movie called *Kung Fu Panda* tells the story of Po, a fictional panda, who works in a noodle shop but becomes a heroic Dragon Warrior.

JACK BLACK

KUNG FU PANDA

21ST-CENTURY PANDA ADDICTION

Efforts to protect the panda in China began in 1957, and the country established its first reserves in 1963. Fast-forward to the 21st century and the world is addicted to pandas. Sixty-four reserves in China are home to wild pandas. Millions of people watch panda cams that broadcast the daily lives of pandas in zoos around the world. A video of a panda sneezing was viewed more than 250 million times on YouTube. When celebrity panda cub Bao Bao (you read about her on page 20) experienced her first snowfall on a winter day in Washington, D.C., in 2015, millions of adoring fans watched her roll down a snowy hill over and over again via the Internet.

Beyond the walls of zoos and the boundaries of forests, the adorable panda is celebrated on souvenirs, statues, emblems, and mass-produced white fuzzy hats with black ears. The image of a panda is used to promote breakfast cereals, carry-out Chinese food, parking garages, and conservation itself. These animals have been fictionalized in movies, cartoons, and television shows.

PANDA HABITAT RECOVERY

How is it that people can love an animal so much, yet leave it nearly homeless? That's what has happened to pandas. The biggest threat to giant pandas, as with many animals around the world, remains the degradation of the species' habitat due to human use over the last few centuries. It's like they live on man-made islands as human activities, such as highway construction, hydropower projects, mining, and farming, cut pandas off from each other. And the slow breeding rate of pandas means it's harder for them to recover from the devastating effects of habitat loss. In addition, climate change could cause changes in bamboo growth.

Historically, China does not have a good track record when it comes to wildlife conservation. In fact, other bears in China, like sun bears and brown bears, don't have the luxury of deep protections like giant pandas. But over the last few decades, scientists and conservation professionals are beginning to help endangered species through a new field called ecological restoration.

Ecological restoration involves hands-on, long-term efforts to work with natural processes to restore an ecosystem that has been degraded or destroyed.

Rescuers are successful in their attempt to save Guo Guo, a giant panda, after a devastating earthquake in China.

IN 2015, PANDA CONSERVATIONISTS IN CHINA RESCUED AND REHABILITATED A SICK WILD PANDA THAT THEY NAMED WOLONG II.

GUO GUO

Panda conservationists consider Guo Guo (GEE-oh GEE-oh) to be a miracle panda after she survived the earthquake that hit her home in the Qionglai mountains at the Wolong Nature Reserve in 2008. That day, the rocks and trees that had provided shelter over Guo Guo's usually quiet enclosure rolled down the mountainside. Guo Guo, 54 days pregnant, scrambled onto a rock that landed in her enclosure. There, she froze.

Later, she and nearly 60 other pandas were evacuated across the Balang and Jiajin mountains to the Bifengxia Panda Center. The earthquake had destroyed the road, leaving rescuers to travel for hours on a treacherous detour. But there was good news ahead: Resilient Guo Guo soon gave birth to healthy twins—the first cubs born after the earthquake.

Years later in 2014, at 16 years old, Guo Guo gave birth to her eighth panda cub. She held it so close that her caregivers had to wait before getting a turn to inspect the baby. This survivor mom is helping her species survive by being an excellent mom. Her new cub may even have a chance for life in the wild.

Taking a photo of my 14-year-old son, Nate, as he had a grand view of panda habitat in the Wolong Nature Reserve. At that moment, I made a commitment to dedicate myself to restoring panda habitat as an example of what well-guided human activity can achieve to restore our fragile world and save endangered species.

Panda biologist Marc Brody and his son, Nate, are all smiles as they hold panda cubs.

MARC BRODY

BORN: LOS ANGELES, CALIFORNIA, U.S.A.
JOB TITLE: FOUNDER AND PRESIDENT OF PANDA MOUNTAIN AND U.S.-CHINA ENVIRONMENTAL FUND
LOCATION: WOLONG NATURE RESERVE IN SICHUAN PROVINCE, SOUTHWEST CHINA
YEARS WORKING WITH PANDAS: 14
MONTHS A YEAR IN THE FIELD: 3

How are you helping to save pandas?
My work focuses on education programs and field work to conserve and restore panda habitat. Conservation protects existing habitat from being degraded. Restoration heals degraded land to become viable habitat in the future. Our organization's work is ensuring that wild pandas have a natural home in which to live.

What's your favorite thing about your job?
I love being in nature and restoring habitat to make our world a better place. At Panda Mountain, we are inspiring, teaching, and training youth on how they can become "positive ecological change agents" to protect nature and wildlands, and conserve endangered species.

What's the best thing about working in the field?
Being in beautiful mountain settings and working with great people that care about our world.

What's the worst thing about working in the field?
A bad day working in the field is still better than a good day in the office. But there *are* leeches that get inside my boots and make my feet bleed and itch.

How can kids prepare to do your job one day?
Get a broad education and learn to respect diverse points of view and different cultures. Habitat conservation is a complex process that requires many interrelated cultural, economic, and political issues to be simultaneously addressed and balanced. This type of work takes an open mind and ability to work well with others.

Panda Mountain director Marc Brody's tips for kids who want to be junior conservationists:

1 Think about what animal, place, or wildlife issue you're most passionate about and learn as much as you can about that topic. Ask questions.

2 Have compassion and empathy for other forms of life. Even a small act like planting a tree will have a positive impact on a place and the animals in it.

3 Share your passion and your success stories! Share good stories about the environment and conservation.

Ecological restoration is the focus of Marc Brody's organization, Panda Mountain, which works in Wolong Nature Reserve, Sichuan Province, in collaboration with local people like Fugui Wan, whom you read about on page 82. Ecological restoration is similar to mass-scale gardening, weeding of non-native plants, and reintroducing native vegetation and reducing overall disturbances to the environment. This is good news for pandas and the other species that share its bamboo forest.

Working closely with the Sichuan government departments, institutes, and universities, scientists like Marc Brody are collaborating to create long-term solutions that will protect pandas and preserve the way of life for neighboring communities. Many people in panda territory are struggling to rebuild their lives after losing their homes and farms to the disastrous earthquake of 2008.

Brody is helping indigenous mountain villagers in protected areas become stewards of the areas in which they live. This way, they are empowered to help restore habitat and protect pandas as they rebuild their own lives.

PANDA IMPOSTERS

People love pandas so much they breed or groom other animals to look like pandas.

A Chinese breed of dog, the chow, looks remarkably like a panda.

Sheep have also been bred to look like pandas.

PANDA CAMP COUNSELOR

At panda camp, biology student Wang Lv Chao is known simply as Alex. He's a beloved volunteer camp counselor who works with children who live in the rural villages adjacent to the giant panda reserves. The kids come to free summer camps at the Chengdu Research Base of Giant Panda Breeding. The program is funded by the United Kingdom's North of England Zoological Society at Chester Zoo.

Even though the children live in rural villages adjacent to the panda reserves, many of them have never seen

a giant panda that lives in the mountains they share. Alex shares his love of animals and nature with the children who come to camp.

Together, they hike mountain paths while Alex teaches them about the importance of China's biodiversity, from giant pandas and bamboo to snakes and rivers. He hopes they share what they've learned with everyone they meet.

At the end of the week, the kids invite their families to an event where they celebrate and share sketches of nature, songs, poems, and plays inspired by what they learned at camp. Kids, he believes, have the power to make the world a better place.

The pied Mexican spiny-tailed iguana is also known as a panda dragon.

A scientist in Washington state, U.S.A., experimented with the breeding of miniature cows to come up with this cuddly panda cow.

MAKE A PLACE GO WILD

Luckily for pandas there are lots of people working hard to help protect them. While most of their habitat has been chopped down, this process is slowly being reversed. Today, many panda habitats are not only being protected, they are being replaced, too. Allowing a wild habitat to replace farm or other land is called rewilding. You may not be able to rewild a whole forest for pandas, but you might be able to rewild a place, whatever the size, in your neighborhood.

ACT

GO WILD.

WORK WITH YOUR SCIENCE TEACHER TO BE SURE THAT YOU HAVE A GOOD LOCATION for your wild project and ask for advice or do your own research on how you can increase the spot's biodiversity. Depending on whether it is a flowerpot, a corner of a garden, or mostly dirt land, the advice will be very different.

TAKE ACTION TO LET THE PLACE GO WILD, BUT BE VERY PATIENT. The process may take weeks and months. The most important thing is to protect the habitat you are helping.

KEEP A RECORD OF THE WAY THAT YOUR LITTLE WILD PLACE CHANGES. Take a photo from the same position every day and you will be able to make a time-lapse movie to reveal the changes.

MAKE

MAP YOUR COMMUNITY.

MAKE A MAP OF PLACES THAT YOU GO TO ON A REGULAR BASIS. This could include your home, school, community, and other spaces. You could draw the map or, with help from a parent, print one from the Internet.

COLOR THE MAP TO SHOW OUTDOOR SPACES that have potential for being even more wild. Roads will have little potential, but you might be able to identify perfectly kept lawns or a place that is unprotected and damaged.

PICK A PLACE THAT YOU THINK HAS GOOD POTENTIAL. Remember, this could be as small as a flowerpot. Get permission from the landowner to look after the space.

"GIANT PANDAS ONLY NEED **ONE THING** FROM HUMANS— THEY NEED US TO FIND **WILLPOWER** TO SAVE SPACE FOR THEM, AND THEN LEAVE THEM **ALONE IN PEACE.**"

—**SARAH BEXELL**, INTERNATIONAL WILDLIFE CONSERVATIONIST

Pandas, like this active cub, love to play in the snow.

IN THAILAND, THE CHIANG MAI ZOO MAKES PAPER FROM FIBER-RICH PANDA POOP.

To prepare for days of panda tracking through mossy, wet panda territory (where it rains or snows about 320 days a year), Ron Swaisgood eats well and gets plenty of sleep. He needs plenty of stamina for long, draining walks up and down slippery ravines in thick bamboo forests.

FACE TO FACE

One morning, Swaisgood hiked up to the top of the ridge near the field station. He heard a commotion in the distance, and thought maybe it was a couple of males fighting for access to a female. Swaisgood took off as fast as he could, slipping and sliding about 1,000 feet (305 m) down into a valley, then back up and down repeatedly. It took about half a day to get where he thought the sound had come from. He looked around but saw nothing.

Disappointed, he sat down on a rock for a drink of water. That's when a panda peeked out from the bamboo about 50 feet (15 m) away from him. The panda then walked toward him, followed by another panda. Their faces were smeared with blood as if they had been fighting. One panda melted back into the bamboo, but the other kept coming. Swaisgood wasn't afraid. Pandas aren't known to have ever attacked a human in the wild. Still, he stood up on the boulder to be safe. The panda backed off a few feet, then disappeared.

Soon it would be dark. Swaisgood needed to get back to the field station. Exhilarated, he ran up and down the steep side of the mountain through dense, dark vegetation. But it was tough going. He tripped and fell onto a jagged bamboo stalk, impaling his eye.

With help from a colleague, he made the difficult walk back to the field station with his eye bleeding. It took days to get to the hospital via truck and airplane, but he and his eyeball made a full recovery.

Despite almost losing an eye that day, Swaisgood has dedicated his career to developing skills as a scientist to help pandas and other endangered animals. His curiosity and dedication keep him motivated, despite the challenges, sacrifices, and risks. He says the reward comes from feeling that what he does will make

PANDA TRAVEL

Whether they are being transported up a mountain, through the forest, or across an ocean, pandas travel in style.

While swapping panda cubs, keepers pass the cubs back and forth in a bucket full of soft, warm towels.

Panda mothers carry their babies in their mouths.

Keepers carry pandas on comfy stretchers if they need to be anesthetized for a medical procedure or an exam.

They get carried up mountains in baskets on their caregivers' backs.

They jet around the world first class as frequent flyers on the Panda Express.

PANDAS INTERNATIONAL

After a trip to the Wolong Giant Panda Breeding Center in 1999, animal lovers Suzanne Braden and Diane Rees were hooked on helping pandas. To help save the endangered species from where they live in Colorado, U.S.A., they co-founded Pandas International (PI). The nonprofit helps the panda centers managed by the China Conservation and Research Center for the Giant Panda by providing medical equipment, supplies, and veterinary medicine. When the rare triplets were born in China in July 2014, for example, PI provided the special formula required to keep the panda cubs fat and happy during their first few months of life.

Kids and families around the world are getting involved with saving pandas through PI's Pennies 4 Pandas program. Kids from all over have donated money raised at birthday parties, lemonade stands, and bake sales to help save pandas. Some kids have even traveled to China with their families to volunteer, with help from PI.

The organization has a strong network of volunteers, like

Karen Wille, who lives in Washington, D.C. Wille is passionate about giant pandas. Her connection with PI has given her a way to channel her passion into tangible ways to help. Since 2009, Wille has been busy helping raise money for the organization. She also writes for PI's blog and has traveled to panda bases and breeding centers in China over the last five years to volunteer as a panda keeper's assistant, cleaning enclosures and helping to feed captive pandas. Despite the hard work (and scooping a lot of panda poop), Wille is grateful for the chance to get involved with saving these precious bears.

a difference in helping endangered species, like pandas, not only survive, but thrive.

Scientists like the ones you've met through the pages of this book are in the trenches of panda conservation. They believe we can save the species. While progress has been made, the species' future is full of challenges. Giant pandas are making a comeback. Can we make it to the finish line?

MAKING A DIFFERENCE

Saving pandas doesn't only happen in zoos and remote mountain panda centers. Scientists and conservationists study pandas in those places, then they take that information and use it as a foundation for conservation work like fund-raising, working with government officials to improve protection laws for both pandas and their forest home, and fighting for things like the limits on logging in China today.

Conservationists like Zhang take it one step further, refining a successful system to breed and train captive pandas to repopulate wild areas with few pandas, and to reintroduce them to areas where pandas can no longer be found at all. So far the rewilding program has released four pandas into the wild, with Tao Tao being

the first. Zhang wants to release pandas every year to improve genetic diversity in wild populations. And he wants to reintroduce giant pandas to places where populations have died out.

SAVING CHINA'S WILD PLACES

Pandas can thrive in the mountainous, cold, wet wilds of China, as long as humans give them space. In 1998, the country implemented logging restrictions that have slowed the destruction of forest land. With the intent of helping pandas find each other from small, far-flung populations, conservationists focus on preserving uninterrupted wildlife corridors so that giant pandas in the wild can find each other to mate.

Some detractors say that too much money goes into panda conservation. But saving pandas also helps save the Earth and other wildlife. Building public support for saving these precious places means restoring green places that help reduce the threat of climate change. In addition, when we save wildlife corridors—where pandas can migrate and mate—we protect snow leopards, mountain sheep, insects, and fungi in one of the most biodiverse regions in the world's temperate forests.

QIANG QIANG

When a wild panda was found starving, weak, and with both rear legs broken in the forest, rescuers from the China Conservation and Research Center for the Giant Panda took action. That day in 2005, they identified the animal as a 20-year-old male and named him Qiang Qiang, which means "strong." The panda was bony and his coat was dull, but vets thought they detected a spark in the panda's eyes.

Wolong Panda Center director Zhang Hemin and his team created an emergency plan to save the panda's life by amputating his legs and then helped him regain his strength through food, water, and a lot of TLC.

Qiang Qiang learned to "walk" by pulling himself with his front claws. He gained weight and strength. His coat regained its shine. Except for his missing limbs, he was the same as any other panda at the center. Until his death in 2015, Qiang Qiang spent his days nibbling bamboo shoots in the shade of Mount Qingcheng's green mountain peaks at the research center.

Organizations like Panda Mountain try to figure out how kids can help save wild places. It is creating ways to connect people to the land and helping them become agents of positive ecological change. It creates opportunities for people to participate hands-on with habitat conservation. The big question is, can we reclaim and reconnect these wild places and give nature a chance to regenerate itself before it's too late?

KIDS HELPING PANDAS

There are no age restrictions on getting in on the action when it comes to helping save an endangered species. Zhang tells a story about a place in Wolong called Lao Ya Shan, which can be translated as "old crow mountain." Not too long ago, a wild panda raided a farmer's cornfield and ate most of the corn. It was a big loss for the farmer. He was angry.

His son, a fifth grader, asked his father not to beat or chase the animal, saying it was their country's national treasure. The son told his father that he'd heard about a program to compensate farmers whose crops had been damaged by wild pandas. On the advice of his teacher, the boy visited his local government office and told the

story. An officer visited the farm and compensated the child's father for his loss.

But you don't have to live in China to help pandas. Fourteen-year-old Carter Ries and 13-year-old Olivia Ries, who live in Fayetteville, Georgia, U.S.A., started an organization called One More Generation (OMG for short) to help save endangered species. They help educate the public and raise money for organizations that help giant pandas, like Pandas International and the World Wildlife Fund. The best part about helping pandas, Carter says, is knowing that his efforts might have helped save an individual animal.

Olivia and Carter hope to one day start the world's largest animal sanctuary to provide a safe haven for many species of endangered animals. For the moment, however, their number one goal is to inspire other kids to stand up and make a difference.

Eleven-year-old Ceci Howes and her little brother, Davey, visited China's Chengdu Research Base of Giant Panda Breeding for a month in 2013. The trip inspired them to help pandas even when they were back at home in Winnipeg, Canada. With help from their friends Emma and Paige Kasian, they have raised and donated more than $1,700 for panda conservation

(continued on page 103)

ANIMAL SUPERPOWERS — VIPs (VERY IMPORTANT PANDAS)

MANY CAPTIVE GIANT PANDAS LIVE LIKE A-LIST CELEBRITIES.

THEY HAVE PRIVATE CHEFS, SERVING THEM ONLY THE FINEST, HEALTHIEST FOODS.

HAPPY BIRTHDAY

FANS AND PAPARAZZI SURROUND THEM TAKING A CONSTANT STREAM OF PHOTOS AND VIDEO.

PEOPLE AROUND THE WORLD CELEBRATE THEIR BIRTHDAYS.

DR. RON SWAISGOOD

BORN: EAST LANSING, MICHIGAN, U.S.A.
JOB TITLE: DIRECTOR OF APPLIED ANIMAL ECOLOGY AND CO-HEAD, GIANT PANDA CONSERVATION UNIT; INSTITUTE FOR CONSERVATION RESEARCH, SAN DIEGO ZOO GLOBAL
LOCATION: SAN DIEGO, CALIFORNIA, U.S.A.
YEARS WORKING WITH PANDAS: 20
MONTHS A YEAR IN THE FIELD: 1–6

How are you helping to save pandas?

For many years, I've worked on the giant panda conservation and breeding program in China. The research I've done with my Chinese colleagues has changed the way pandas are managed, and that has been part of the reason why we've had an explosion in breeding at the Wolong Panda Center. I also study panda ecology, like available den sites and the types of bamboo growing in the panda reserves. The health of these things lets us know if the habitat will support successful breeding of pandas.

What's your favorite thing about your job?

The main thing is getting to be the "boots on the ground" on projects all over the world, including tracking giant pandas in the mountain forests of China. I also like helping the San Diego Zoo grow and change directions to better meet the needs of conservation.

What's the best thing about working in the field?

When you see a giant panda, it's a special event. We can easily find the ones we have collared, but it's the effort and mystery that goes into panda research that makes seeing a panda in the wild exciting.

What's the worst thing about working in the field?

With pandas, it's the thing that they love most—the bamboo. Beating your way through that thick, thick bamboo is brutal, like a wet, cold carpet of grass that's higher than your head.

How can kids prepare to do your job one day?

My job is all about curiosity. My advice to kids is to always follow their curiosity about nature.

A panda enjoys a bite of bamboo.

The first time I ever saw a wild panda. I had been studying pandas in the field for more than a year. I had seen a lot of panda droppings and a lot of teeth bite marks on leftover bamboo stumps, but I had never seen a panda in the wild until that moment. It was thrilling.

PAPIER MÂCHÉ PANDA ARMY >>>

In 2014, 1,600 giant pandas crowded into the Hong Kong Airport. Each one of the papier mâché pieces of artwork represented a panda alive in the wild. Their creator, French artist Paulo Grangeon, hopes that the impact of his pandas will help people realize how few pandas survive in the wild today.

The 1,600 Paper Pandas Exhibition was launched by Grangeon and the World Wildlife Fund in 2008 to promote conservation of wild pandas and their habitat. The handmade paper pandas were crafted from recycled paper. Each one stands between 5 and 18 inches (12.7 and 45.7 cm) high. Some sit and others stand on all fours. One is even reading a tiny Chinese newspaper. Before arriving in Hong Kong, the pandas toured Europe (at right, seen at the Eiffel Tower in Paris, France). In Germany fans set up a "hospital" to repair pandas that needed a touch-up with black and white tape.

The little pandas also spent time in Taiwan, where crowds waited for hours to take pictures of them, causing a social media frenzy.

by setting up their yard like a Sichuan teahouse. They also sponsored a panda named Xue Xue. But they like to remind people that it's not enough to sell Chinese tea, cookies, and panda items and donate the earnings. They say—if you want to save pandas, each of us has to think about the way we treat the environment we all share, and do a better job.

Kids who want to save pandas believe that endangered species like giant pandas have as much right to live on Earth as humans do, and that our own survival on this planet is directly tied to the well-being of all species. It's about sharing the Earth and keeping it healthy.

GET INVOLVED!

These kids took action—so can you! Helping pandas takes research, creativity, and passion. Talk to your family and everyone who will listen to what you have learned about giant pandas. Swaisgood says the most important thing kids can do to help is to get outside and fall in love with nature. We won't have a next generation of environmental champions unless kids get out and explore nature, and fall in love with it along the way.

To learn more about wildlife conservation, do your research. Get information from reputable resources like Pandas International, World Wildlife Fund, the IUCN, and the National Geographic Society. Check your facts with multiple sources.

Simple action can reduce the pressure on the natural resources that we share with pandas. Pick up litter in your neighborhood or at your school, turn off the water while you brush your teeth, keep lights turned off, and eat local food. You have also probably heard the saying "reduce, reuse, recycle." It is an important reminder that every little bit helps. Endangered Species Day—celebrated on the third Friday in May—is also a great time to raise awareness in your community about giant pandas and other endangered species.

Take action today. Even a small change done every day, every week, or every month adds up. Getting involved with improving our world—and the giant pandas in it—will become a habit you won't want to break. By reading this book, you've already started your own mission panda rescue!

>> EXPERT TIPS

Carter and Olivia Ries's tips for saving endangered pandas:

1 Donate money or time to organizations dedicated to protecting endangered pandas, like Pandas International.

2 Sponsor or adopt a panda at a zoo as a gift for a friend.

3 Buy products from companies that donate money to panda conservation.

Carter and Olivia Ries pass on their panda knowledge to other kids to help save the endangered giant panda species.

>> RESCUE ACTIVITIES

PARTY LIKE A PANDA

People like great news. The good news is that while pandas need protecting, their habitat is slowly making a comeback. Because people care about them, their numbers are slowly increasing, too. That is good news to celebrate, but there is a lot more work still to be done. Many species of wildlife around the world are on the brink of extinction and they need people like you to take action to save them. To celebrate small successes and raise support for more, let's party like pandas!

ACT

MOVE LIKE A PANDA.

INVITE EVERYONE TO COME DRESSED AS PANDAS At a minimum, all guests could be asked to wear black and white clothes. Or they could wear panda eye patches.

DANCE LIKE A PANDA TO PANDA-STYLE MUSIC Are there any songs about pandas, or do any artists sing about black and white? Make sure to play them!

HOLD A PANDA COMPETITION WITH PRIZES You could award people for the best costume, dance, panda puppet, or panda impressions.

MAKE

ORGANIZE A PANDA DANCE PARTY.

FIND A GREAT PLACE TO HOLD A PANDA DANCE PARTY You will need to get permission from your parents, guardians, or school to use a space.

MAKE POSTERS, INVITATIONS, AND TICKETS FOR YOUR EVENT Sell tickets to the party to raise funds to help protect endangered species.

PLAN EVERYTHING YOU NEED TO MAKE THE PARTY A SUCCESS Think about how the venue should be decorated, what music you will have, any food or drink needed, and what games you might play.

SHARE

MAKE MORE NOISE.

CHALLENGE EVERYONE AT THE PARTY TO DO AT LEAST ONE THING TO HELP and other endangered species. You could ask them to make a donation to a wildlife charity or sign a petition you have organized.

If you invite them, they may send a photographer to take pictures of you dressed up as a panda. Be sure to tell them the serious purpose of the party.

Everyone could pay $1 to make and wear panda eye patches for the day. All of the money you raise can be added to the funds raised at your panda party.

BECOME AN EXPERT

Partying like a panda is fun, and so is working with pandas! From photographers to geographers, there are lots of different experts who work to understand and protect pandas. Study well, and in the future you could work with endangered species and help their survival into the future.

ECOLOGIST
Ecologists are scientists who study the relationships between different animals and the environments they live in.

CARTOGRAPHER
Cartographers make maps that show where pandas are and how the shape of their habitat is changing.

CAMPAIGNER
If you have been doing the activities in this book you are already a campaigner! Keep going and you might get paid to do this job in the future.

Returning pandas to the wild will help the next generation of pandas survive.

CONCLUSION

RELEASE DAY

At the edge of the bamboo forest in the Liziping Nature Reserve in Sichuan, preparations are under way for an elaborate release ceremony. The celebration involves dancers, news crews, and a quarter-mile (0.4 km) of red carpet so that the many dignitaries and politicians at the event won't slip in the cold mud or get their shoes dirty. The deciduous trees in the forest have turned to beautiful hues of red, yellow, and orange. Although he may not know it, Tao Tao's been training for this moment for his entire life. He's ready for the mission.

The crate door opens. A wall of bamboo shields him from the sight of humans. But the sounds give him a fright—it's a fear that will serve him well in the wild.

Despite their worries, Tao Tao's caregivers stay optimistic about his ability to survive and to help repopulate pandas in the wild with a new bloodline.

He hesitates first inside his crate, and then takes a few slow steps. Then he runs for the bamboo forest, his rear end disappearing into the dense underbrush of the forest. As he goes, he breaks free from the boundaries of captivity to live in the wild.

A YEAR LATER

A year later, no one has seen Tao Tao since his release day. But his GPS collar shows that he is alive and well, roaming the misty mountains and crossing rocky, rippling mountain streams like any wild panda would. Zhang reports that Tao Tao's activity zone is large. He has established his own home range. Maybe he's met others. Maybe he's fathered a wild cub of his own. In 2015, reports indicate that Tao Tao is healthy and active.

In his documentary *Pandas: The Journey Home*, Nicolas Brown tells the story of Tao Tao's release and follows the lives of several pandas at Wolong. He also shows the lives and struggles of the people who care for the pandas, like Zhang. Zhang believes Tao Tao's first steps into the wild, like man's historic first steps on the moon, are an historic moment for panda conservation.

RESOURCES

WANT TO LEARN MORE?

Check out these great resources to continue your mission to save giant pandas!

IN PRINT

Jazynka, Kitson. **"Panda Party."** *National Geographic Kids* (March 2014), 14–17.

Musgrave, Ruth A. **"Bamboozled."** *National Geographic Kids* (June/July 2008), 30–31.

Musgrave, Ruth A. **"Panda Shake-Up."** *National Geographic Kids* (December 2010/January 2011), 22–23.

Schaller, George. ***Giant Pandas in the Wild.*** Aperture Foundation, 2002.

Schreiber, Anne. ***National Geographic Readers: Pandas.*** National Geographic Society, 2010.

Zhihe, Zhang, and Sarah M. Bexell. ***Giant Pandas: Born Survivors.*** Penguin Books China, 2012.

ONLINE

Chengdu Research Base of Giant Panda Breeding
Conducts research, breeds giant pandas, and promotes conservation education to protect giant pandas
panda.org.cn

Defenders of Wildlife
Protects animals and their habitats around the world
defenders.org

International Union for Conservation of Nature
Assesses and compiles a list of threatened species around the world; provides information on the state of giant pandas
iucnredlist.org

National Geographic Education
Information about history, science, animals, and more
nationalgeographic.com/education

National Geographic Kids
Provides information on animals from around the world
nationalgeographic.com/kids/animals

National Wildlife Federation
Protects wildlife in the United States
nwf.org

Panda Mountain
Working to restore panda habitat
uscef.org

Pandas International
Promotes public awareness about giant pandas
pandasinternational.org

San Diego Zoo Global
A conservation organization dedicated to the science of saving endangered species worldwide
sandiegozooglobal.org

Smithsonian's National Zoo
A leader in science and wildlife preservation and public education
nationalzoo.si.edu

World Wildlife Fund
Promotes people living in harmony with wildlife around the world
wwf.org

Zoo Atlanta
Dedicated to the preservation of wildlife
zooatlanta.org

WATCH

"Earth, Episode One: Home." *Earth a New Wild.* PBS, 2014.

Pandas: The Journey Home. National Geographic, 2014.

Save the Panda. National Geographic, 1983.

SELECT SCIENTIFIC PAPERS

Bexell, Sarah. "The Importance of Environmental Education for Young Children." *Green Tianfu Education Journal* (119)2, (2010), 51–52. (In Chinese, translation by Feng Rui Xi).

DingZhen, Liu, Wei RongPing, Zhang GuiQuan, Yuan Hong, Wang ZhiPeng, Sun Lixing, Zhang JianXu, and Zhang Hemin. "Male Panda Urine Contains Kinship Information." *Chinese Science Bulletin* 53, no. 18, 2793–2800. DOI:10.1007/s11434-008-0373-7.

Dungl, Eveline, Dagmar Schratter, and Ludwig Huber. "Discrimination of Face-Like Patterns in the Giant Panda." *Journal of Comparative Psychology* 11, no. 4 (2008), 335–343. DOI: 10.1037/0735-7036.122.4.335.

Ouyang, Zhiyun, Liu Jianguo Liu, and Zhang Hemin. "Giant panda habitat community structure in Wolong Nature Reserve, China." *Acta Ecologica Sinica* 20(3) (2000), 458–462.

Swaisgood, Ronald R., Fuwen Wei, David E. Wildt, Andrew J. Kouba, and Zejun Zhang. "Giant Panda Conservation Science: How Far We Have Come." *Biology Letters* 11, no. 2 (February 2015). DOI: 10.1098/rsbl.2009.0786.

ORGANIZATIONS IN THIS BOOK

Association of Zoos and Aquariums
aza.org

Bifengxia Panda Base
giantpandazoo.com/panda/china/ccrcgp/bfx

Chengdu Research Base of Giant Panda Breeding
panda.org.cn

Chimelong Safari Park, Guangzhou, China
chimelong.com

China Conservation and Research Center for the Giant Panda
chinapanda.org.cn

China's Department of Forestry
english.forestry.gov.cn

The Field Museum of Natural History
fieldmuseum.org

International Union for Conservation of Nature (IUCN)
iucnredlist.org

North of England Zoological Society at Chester Zoo
chesterzoo.org

One More Generation
onemoregeneration.org

Panda Mountain
uscef.org

Pandas International
pandasinternational.org

San Diego Zoo Global
sandiegozooglobal.org

Smithsonian's National Zoo
nationalzoo.si.edu

World Wildlife Fund
wwf.org

Zoo Atlanta
zooatlanta.org

PLACES TO SEE PANDAS AROUND THE WORLD

Adelaide Zoo, Australia
Beijing Zoo, Beijing, China
Changsha Zoo, China
Chapultepec Zoo, Mexico City, Mexico
Chengdu Research Base of Giant Panda Breeding, and Zoo, Chengdu, China
Chiang Mai Zoo, Thailand
Chimelong Safari Park, Guangzhou, China
China Conservation and Research Center for the Giant Panda, Bifengxia Panda Base, Ya'an City, China
Liziping Nature Reserve, Shimian, China
Luoguantai Wildlife Rescue Center, Xi'an, China
Memphis Zoo, Tennessee, U.S.A.
Ocean Park, Hong Kong, China
Oji Zoo, Kobe, Japan
San Diego Zoo, California, U.S.A.
Schönbrunn Zoo, Vienna, Austria
Seven Star Park Zoo, Guilin, China
Smithsonian's National Zoo, Washington, D.C., U.S.A.
Ueno Zoo, Toyko, Japan
Zoo Atlanta, Georgia, U.S.A.

INDEX

Boldface indicates illustrations.

CREDITS

From page 7: $10.00 donation to National Geographic Society. Charges will appear on your wireless bill or be deducted from your prepaid balance. All purchases must be authorized by account holder. Must be 18 years of age or have parental permission to participate. Message and data rates may apply. Text STOP to 50555 to STOP. Text HELP to 50555 for HELP. Full terms: www.mGive.org/T

Dedication

For all the kids who love giant pandas enough to help save them. We have so much to learn from these amazing animals! —KJ

For all pandas. —DRE

Special Thanks

To Dr. Rebecca Snyder, Dr. Ron Swaisgood, Nic Brown, Zhang Hemin, Jade Xia, Marc Brody, Suzanne Braden, Dr. Sarah Bexell, James Cahill and all of the experts who helped me while I was working on this panda project. Without your passion, insights, expertise, and the willingness to share your stories, this book would not have been possible.

To Kate Olesin for entrusting me with the project, and to Daniel Raven-Ellison, Christy Ullrich Barcus, Lori Epstein, Angela Modany, and the entire National Geographic Children's Books team who helped create this book.

—Kitson Jazynka

Staff for this book

Kate Olesin, Editor
Christy Ullrich Barcus, Project Editor
Jülide Obuz Dengel, Art Director
Graves Fowler Creative, Designer
Lori Epstein, Senior Photo Editor
Debbie Gibbons, Director of Intracompany Cartography
Greg Ugiansky, Map Research and Production
Paige Towler, Editorial Assistant
Sanjida Rashid and Rachel Kenny, Design Production Assistants
Tammi Colleary-Loach, Rights Clearance Manager
Michael Cassady and Mari Robinson, Rights Clearance Specialists
Grace Hill, Managing Editor
Joan Gossett, Senior Production Editor
Lewis R. Bassford, Production Manager
Rachel Faulise, Manager, Production Services
Susan Borke, Legal and Business Affairs
Rebekah Cain, Imaging

Published by the National Geographic Society

Gary E. Knell, President and CEO
John M. Fahey, Chairman of the Board
Melina Gerosa Bellows, Chief Education Officer
Declan Moore, Chief Media Officer
Hector Sierra, Senior Vice President and General Manager, Book Division

Senior Management Team

Kids Publishing and Media; Nancy Laties Feresten, Senior Vice President; Erica Green, Vice President, Editorial Director, Kids Books; Jennifer Emmett, Vice President, Content; Eva Absher-Schantz, Vice President, Visual Identity; Rachel Buchholz, Editor and Vice President, *NG Kids* magazine; Jay Sumner, Photo Director; Amanda Larsen, Design Director, Kids Books; Hannah August, Marketing Director; R. Gary Colbert, Production Director

Digital

Laura Goertzel, Manager; Sara Zeglin, Senior Producer; Bianca Bowman, Assistant Producer; Natalie Jones, Senior Product Manager

The National Geographic Society is one of the world's largest nonprofit scientific and educational organizations. Founded in 1888 to "increase and diffuse geographic knowledge," the Society's mission is to inspire people to care about the planet. It reaches more than 400 million people worldwide each month through its official journal, *National Geographic,* and other magazines; National Geographic Channel; television documentaries; music; radio; films; books; DVDs; maps; exhibitions; live events; school publishing programs; interactive media; and merchandise. National Geographic has funded more than 10,000 scientific research, conservation, and exploration projects and supports an education program promoting geographic literacy.

For more information, please visit nationalgeographic.com, call 1-800-NGS LINE (647-5463), or write to the following address:
National Geographic Society
1145 17th Street N.W.
Washington, D.C. 20036-4688 U.S.A.

Visit us online at nationalgeographic.com/books

For librarians and teachers: ngchildrensbooks.org

More for kids from National Geographic: kids.nationalgeographic.com

For information about special discounts for bulk purchases, please contact National Geographic Books Special Sales: ngspecsales@ngs.org

For rights or permissions inquiries, please contact National Geographic Books Subsidiary Rights: ngbookrights@ngs.org

Trade paperback ISBN: 978-1-4263-2088-0
Reinforced library binding: 978-1-4263-2089-7

Printed in Hong Kong
15/THK/1